BE
ING
AS
LEAD
ING

YOUR ROADMAP TO SHAPING CULTURE THROUGH LIFE'S DISRUPTIONS

DR.KENDRA MOMON

AVAIL

Being As Leading: Your Roadmap to Shaping Culture Through Life's Disruptions
copyright ©2020 Dr. Kendra Momon

ISBN: 978-1-950718-62-7

Printed in the United States of America
cover design by Joe Deleon

Avail
225 W. Seminole Blvd., Suite 105
Sanford, FL 32771

CONTENTS

DEDICATION

I'd like to dedicate this book to all of the leaders in my life—past, present, and future—who modeled, encouraged, and even challenged me to be all that God called and created me to be. Without your intentional mentorship, guidance, love, and correction, I don't know if I would have naturally risen to the occasion to develop, grow, download, and multiply myself into others and embrace the fullness of the *Imago Dei* and my destiny. Any fruit that remains in my life should be attributed to your instruction and training. Thank you for allowing me to be as I learned how to lead.

ACKNOWLEDGMENTS

To my husband, pastor, trainer, coach, chief encourager, and #1 supporter, Andrew (Mo) L. Momon, Jr., Thank you for believing in me, speaking up for me, leading me, championing me and ALWAYS praying for me. Thank you for modeling servant-leadership, compassion, and conviction in public and—most importantly—in private. I am better because of you and stronger too #momonstrongforlife. I love you.

To my mom, Jacquelyn, Early on, you instilled generosity and integrity in me. While you played absolutely no games and I have to remember I'm an adult when you use that "tone of voice," I am indebted to you. Your sacrifice—even when it has been painful, isolating, and inconvenient—is the foundation on which I stand. Thank you and bless you. I love you.

Lastly, to all my family, friends, colleagues, leaders, and comrades in the faith who in any way—large or small—have added value to my life and directly or indirectly contributed to the writing of this book, Thank you!

INTRODUCTION

MY FONDEST MEMORIES growing up are the times I spent at my grandmother's house. While I lived two doors down from her, there was nothing like the up-close-and-personal actions my little observant mind witnessed at her leadership helm.

I guess I should mention that Nana, as we affectionately called her, was also our neighborhood "candy lady." Given her "rep" as always having the best supply of Swedish fish, Now and Laters, sunflower seeds and bubble gum, I instantaneously was the recipient of "street cred" (a quality that makes you likely to be accepted by ordinary young people who live in towns and cities because you have the same fashions, styles, interests, culture or opinions).

Whether it was walking home from school with my cousins or up the block to go to one of my aunties' houses, I was affectionately known as one of Mrs. Logan's grandkids. That translated to, "She's cool; don't mess with her." Nana's reputation became a badge of protection for me as I tried my best to manage the sometimes hectic and, at times, painfully awkward elementary and middle school years of my life as an introverted, overachieving and—by the time I entered sixth grade—size 8.5 shoe wearer.

Wearing a size 8.5 shoe and being called "Can't Dance" and "Klondike" weren't the only painful transitions that happened during this time. My mom and I also moved to a new neighborhood about 10 minutes away from Nana's protective covering. The new neighborhood didn't have a "candy lady." It had a corner store, and Mr. Arnold apparently skipped Customer Service 101.

The new neighborhood, while nicer than our old one, also had its share of middle-school bullies and mean girls, as well as economic, social and even racial divides. I'd lie if I said there weren't times that I wished we'd just move back to Chad Brown, my beloved childhood neighborhood. Other than my uncle, aunt, and five cousins who moved to the East Side at the same time we did, the only other thing I liked about the move was my sixth grade English and history teachers, Mrs. Cooley and Mrs. Zexter.

As I began to slowly accept that I wasn't going to be Dorothy, click my Airmax 95s two times, and be back in my preferred neighborhood, I started to think about how I could not just survive but thrive in my new normal. While at the time I didn't know this was where my journey and passion for "being as leading" was birthed, these crucial years were when I developed both survival skills and strategic-thinking skills. Both helped ease the internal conflicts that abounded between who I knew I could be and how I kept showing up.

Reflecting back, even through the tears, I know that I failed to operate in being as leading. I was more concerned about not rocking the boat and "going along to get along" than being true to the beat of my heart.

As a result, my formative thinking processes about being as leading were full of failed bargaining techniques and flat-out defeats.

CASE STUDY #1—BEING BULLIED ISN'T LEADING

One of the things I learned early on in my new neighborhood is that if the teacher praised you and said anything about your smarts, you became a target. Let's just say Mrs. Cooley put a "NEW HERE" neon green target on my back in English class. Being a transfer student, the new school didn't believe that I was on the reading level stated by my old school, so I was not put in the appropriate reading class. While in Mrs. Cooley's class, everyone else was on reading level 12 or 13, and I was on level 17. As a result, while others struggled through the two-hour period, I didn't and used the time to read some of my favorite non-textbooks and magazines.

One day a young lady—who shall remain nameless—cornered me and told me that from now on I'd be doing her homework too or be at the wrath of her fists. Being the brave warrior I was (absolutely not), I took on this brazen demand. For three months, I struggled in silence staying up into the late hours of the evening finishing chores, then doing my homework—followed by her homework.

I'll never forget the night my mom inquired as to why it was taking me so long to do homework when it had never been the case for me before. I remember like it was yesterday as the first few tears of stress, fear and weariness rolled down my face. With my head slightly bowed, I began to tell my mom of the unreasonable, non-negotiable situation I had found myself in: do her homework or get beat down by her fists.

The look of shock on her face, coupled with a few colorful words, led to a meeting with the school principal during which my mom did two things. First, she called for a prompt end to the bullying. Second, she notified the homework bully's parents. That problem was over! While this story had a somewhat happy ending (externally, everything was resolved), internally, I began to question myself and what caused me to fail to be the leader my mom had raised me to be. And, I made a decision that I would never allow myself to be forced into telling the truth or leading.

CASE STUDY #2—BEING ONE WHO GOES ALONG TO GET ALONG ISN'T LEADING

I wish I could tell you that the sixth grade was the only time I compromised who I was in order to go along to get along and not get beat up, but sadly it wasn't. Fast-forward to my first professorship at one of our nation's beloved football schools in the South.

While I graduated with my Ph.D. in Political Science from The Ohio State University, which is also a large research school and football-loving institution, the stakes were different as I navigated the terrain from a graduate student to an actual employee. As an employee, especially at a state-funded institution, I was very aware of which lines a person must not cross as they relate to the separation of church and state and the First Amendment.

Being one whose personality profile and Enneagram numbers indicate a strong penchant to color within the lines, I found myself in numerous uncomfortable positions as Holy Spirit would speak to my spirit during lectures on political parties, interest groups and civil liberties. Often, I would ignore Him and power through the lectures because I understood that, while I was a Christian by confession, I was a political scientist by profession, and I needed to keep my job—so I thought.

One day, in the middle of February, I was delivering a lecture on federalism. With about 325 out of the 400 students in Introduction to American Government present, and my six teaching assistants front and center, I mounted the platform with my laptop and headset microphone ready to go, when I first felt the strong prompting to share a message that had bubbled up in my spirit.

As usual, I knew the game plan: go along to get along (i.e. ignore Him). 15 minutes into the lecture, as I was breaking down the various types of federalism—dualism, cooperative, *laissez-faire*—I felt His presence again and heard a message that I couldn't ignore. So with some shaking in my voice, I began to address the class. I stepped out from behind the lectern and delivered the download I had received.

First, let me apologize in advance, but I need to interrupt lecture because I can't shake or continue to ignore what I'm hearing, I said. God says there is someone here this morning who is contemplating suicide. You are going to take your life, and He is saying, "Do not do it. He loves you, and He cares for you!"

I don't remember much about the day after that other than praying I didn't receive a call to go see the dean. Two days later, I did receive a call, however. Someone left a message on my office phone and said, "Dr. King (my maiden name), it was me that you were talking to in the lecture. I was going to take my life, but because of what you shared, I am not going to do it. Thank you for interrupting lecture for me."

On that day, being a go-along-to-get-along, color-by-number, draw-within-the-lines leader was laid to rest as my core understanding of who God has wired me to be was tested and resurrected in power.

CASE STUDY #3—BEING AS LEADING

In his book, True North, Bill George writes about defining moments that shape us as leaders. These crucible moments, if utilized well, point us in the direction of our "True North"—who we are at our core.

In the Bible, we encounter so many who have defining crucible moments: Daniel in the lions' den and Esther in the king's court, to name a couple. What's interesting is that, in these instances, both Daniel and Esther got to a place at which they made the tough decision to not bow, ultimately declaring, "If I perish, I perish."

The poet William Cullen Bryant said it this way: "Truth crushed to the earth will rise again."

Dr. Martin Luther King, Jr., said it this way: "The ultimate measure of a man is not where he stands in moments of comfort and convenience, but where he stands at times of challenge and controversy."

Brené Brown says it this way: "Integrity is choosing courage over comfort."

And, the wisest of them all, Jesus, said it this way: "Greater love has no one than this: to lay down one's life for one's friends" (John 15:13, NIV).

Do you see the pattern yet? In and of ourselves, we aren't equipped to wholeheartedly lead from the place of our being.

First, it can be difficult to arrive at a place where being is leading because so many of us aren't fully aware of who God says we are and who He ordained us to be. Yes, we know the Word. We can equip and empower others. Yet, do we truly believe this truth?

You have searched me, LORD, and you know me. You know when I sit and when I rise; you perceive my thoughts from afar. You discern my going out and my lying down; you are familiar with all my ways. Before a word is on my tongue you, LORD, know it completely. You hem me in behind and before, and you lay your hand upon me. —Psalm 139:1-5 (NIV)

Know this: Who you are—how you process, think and are uniquely wired—is all a part of the divine intricacies of the power, presence and purposes of God in your life. The insight, opportunities and revelation that only seem to come your way are all mechanisms He has equipped you with to walk out leading from being.

The reality, however, is that as I shared in my first two case studies, like the younger me, so many of us are failing to lead from a place of being because we aren't yet aware of, in touch with, or confident about the true essence of who God says we are to be.

We aren't being in our leading because we are trying to lead devoid of our fundamental core values, non-negotiables and beliefs. Being is the nature or lifeblood of a person. It is a state of mind. It is the collection of thoughts and perspectives we possess. It is a place or position. It is oneness.

In a world that constantly bombards us with symbols, thoughts, images, language and even emojis that tell us who we ought to be, how often do we find ourselves—even as believers—succumbing to society's accepted values for living, leading and being to the detriment of our faith-filled beliefs?

If we are going to walk in the power of being as leading, where the full essence of who God has wired us to be shows up, we have to ask some questions:

1. Who are you when you are being?

2. Is who you are when you are being different than who you are when you are leading?

3. Can your being stand alone and be at peace when you aren't leading?

As you can tell, all of these being as leading questions center on one's identity, and until we are clear that, "God said it. I believe it. That settles it. Amen!" we will never be able to fully lead from a place of transparency, vulnerability, honesty and empathy. Instead of being in our leading, we may find ourselves in a state of being in which we erroneously adhere to broken, antiquated and even patriarchal models of leading. You know them. They are models that adhere to false narratives of leadership such as the following:

"You've got to be stern if you are going to lead."

"Women are too emotional to lead."

"Millennials are terrible leaders."

"You can't trust the people you lead."

"There is no such thing as team in leading."

Maybe you haven't heard those exact sentiments, but you were raised to believe that you've got to be micromanaging to lead. Maybe you were raised to believe that you've got to be demanding and unapologetic to lead. Maybe you believe that, based on societal influences, only certain races and cultures are equipped to lead.

It really doesn't matter what you may have believed. The truth of the matter is that we all have an opportunity to walk in the power of being as leading because delay isn't denial. What we may have forfeited before in our leadership (which I define as the ability to influence people, environments and outcomes towards the achievement of a collective goal) doesn't have the final word in our lives. Moreover, what we have believed about leadership in an old season doesn't have to be our constant companion in this new season. As Paul reminds us,

> Therefore, if anyone is in Christ, the new creation has come: The old has gone, the new is here! All this is from God, who reconciled us to himself through Christ and gave us the ministry of reconciliation: that God was reconciling the world to himself in Christ, not counting people's sins against them. And he has committed to us the message of reconciliation.
> —2 Corinthians 5:17-19 (NIV)

If the coronavirus pandemic has taught us anything, I believe it's that the greatest leaders among us are those who are serving on the front lines in a broad range of low-end and high-profile industries of which we were all guilty of taking for granted. Every time our cashiers, bus drivers, EMTs, medical doctors, government officials and faith-based leaders show up, we ought to thank them for their service—for their examples of being as leading.

I like how Dr. King said it: "Everybody can be great... because anybody can serve. You don't have to have a college degree to serve. You don't have to make your subject and verb agree to serve. You only need a heart full of grace. A soul generated by love."

In this season, ask yourself, Who is God calling me to be? Am I being in my leading or is this an opportunity for me to evolve into His leadership vision of me—predestined since He created me?

Remember, there is another you inside of you, desirous to lead from a place of being present in His presence, from a place of wholeheartedness, and from a place of oneness where your literal being leads.

chapter 1

REWIND

DO YOU KNOW what Merriam-Webster's 2014 Word of the Year happened to be? When I was wondering about this, off the top of my head, I didn't. What I found out, is that while there were a lot of unique, compelling, and even racy words—insidious, legacy, feminism, and *je ne sais quoi* made the top 10 list—the number one choice was "culture." More people looked up and searched for it at Merriam-Webster.com than any other word. Reflecting back on 2014, I couldn't help but ask why there was such a need to understand the ethos, logos, and pathos of a word that has been in the American lexicon for centuries. In examining some of the top trends of 2014, I found that Gallup.com listed Americans' foremost concerns. The leadership of former President Barack Obama, policy decisions of the U.S. Congress, unemployment, and healthcare topped the list.

The year 2014 was also a year during which polarizing issues—war, pestilence, political upheaval, police brutality, legalization of marijuana and mass street protests—consumed national and international consciousness. The irony about these news stories is that they didn't have to do anything to get the spotlight. The mere presence of these issues and what they represented to so many deemed them significant enough to be front-page news. More troubling than the political issues of 2014, were the repeated incidents of "man's inhumanity to man." It was the year that the ability of some groups of people to walk in the fullness of the *Imago Dei* was challenged, attacked, and even violently stolen.

Most notably, 2014 was the year that the nation and the world heard a video recording of Eric Garner—an unarmed black man—gasp, "I can't breathe," shortly before being murdered by a law enforcement induced choke hold. He was killed—both figuratively and literally—at the hands of the NYPD.

FAST-FORWARD

2020 has brought killer dust clouds, murdering bees, an international pandemic, food-supply shortages, and another unarmed black man—George Floyd—uttering the words, "I can't breathe," while being held down by three police officers for 8 minutes and 46 seconds until he took his last gasp of air. In one of the most inhumane and despicably horrific acts of violence witnessed in the 21st century, Mr. Floyd pleaded, "I can't breathe," over 20 times only to be told by Minneapolis police officer Derek Chauvin, "It takes a heck of a lot of oxygen to talk." This brazen disregard for the *Imago Dei* is another painful example of the cruel and unusual punishment the 8th Amendment is supposed to protect Americans against. Yet, here we are six years later in what seems to be a repeat—on steroids—of 2014.

It's no secret that six years ago the statement, "I can't breathe," appeared to fall on culturally tone-deaf ears. While people were upset, there was no on-going outrage or demand for change. If we can be completely honest, some people blamed Eric Garner by saying he should have complied with police. Today, however, "I can't breathe," has become an impetus for overdue economic, political, social-justice, and legislative change. In a mixed bag of sadness and anger, with an ironic silver lining, "I can't breathe," has also become an international clarion call that is transcending traditional political dividers and focusing the spotlight on those who wield power absent of love, justice, humility, and grace. Still, the question remains, "How can I be all that the Creator made me to be if immutable characteristics—for example, skin color—subject me to others who refuse to acknowledge my humanity?"

BE[ING]

The word "be" is derived from the Old English word *beon* which means "to exist, happen, or come to be." In addition to its primary definition, it also means "to take place, to occupy a place or position, to continue, to remain, and to operate." The Cambridge Dictionary describes it in multiple contexts including the use of the word being which means "the state of existence." Be connotes the nature or essence of something and speaks to a real or living creation as in a human being. For me, being is the substance and essence of who a person is in the *Imago Dei*. It is a person's authentic self, core values, and wiring—a conglomeration of one's non-negotiables, one's "I know that I know that I know" self, one's intuition, and one's discernment. Another way to think about it is that being is the sum total of one's thoughts, personal and life experiences, and relationship with oneself and others.

Being is a state of mind, a vibe, a combination of one's perspective, passion, and purpose from the inside out. Being can also mean embracing who God says you are, pursuing His will for your life, and thriving—not striving—in His promises and plans. In a society where culture is seemingly louder and more convincing than the simplicity of life in Christ, it is important to know the importance of being in Him. Time and time again, Scripture makes it clear that a person's identity is found in his or her being in Him—not doing in Him. In spite of this piercing truth, many of us find ourselves in modern-day Martha and Mary role reversals. We get so consumed by our fast-paced, quick-fix, hurry-up-and-wait, 100 mph consumer culture that our to-do lists lead us. Here is a friendly PSA: In Him we live, move, and have our being. When we remember this truth, our being as leading will emanate from who we are and not what we do.

Let me be clear: What we do is important. However, our doing in Him should never override our being in Him. By way of reminder, let's look at the story of two sisters: Martha and Mary. It's a classic tale of doing versus being.

As Jesus and the disciples continued on their way to Jerusalem, they came to a certain village where a woman named Martha welcomed him into her home. Her sister, Mary, sat at the Lord's feet, listening to what he taught. But Martha was distracted by the big dinner she was preparing.

She came to Jesus and said, "Lord, doesn't it seem unfair to you that my sister just sits here while I do all the work? Tell her to come and help me." But the Lord said to her, "My dear Martha, you are worried and upset over all these details! There is only one thing worth being concerned about. Mary has discovered it, and it will not be taken away from her." — Luke 10:38-42 (NLT)

I wonder how many rebukes Jesus would have to issue today to all of the modern day, 21st century 2020 Marthas who are "doing the most" being consumed by doing the work of ministry rather than just being and resting in the power, purpose, and presence of the One in whom we are supposed to live, move, and have our being? You know what the church mothers would say: "If you can't say, 'Amen,' say, 'Ouch.'"

BE STILL AND KNOW

Be still and know. Maybe you need to slow down and read it again. BE STILL AND KNOW! Take a breath, pause, slow down, or just chill. Read it again, but this time say it out loud—BE STILL AND KNOW. Be still and know that I am God! I will be honored by every nation. I will be honored throughout the world. —Psalm 46:10 (NLT)

What a powerful reminder and pregnant pause for us all to heed. Truthfully, it can be hard to do this because we live in a culture that tells us we don't have time to slow down—let alone be still and know. Yet, in that passage of scripture, God is saying,

"Settle yourself." To me, He is saying, "Hey, you. Yes, you with your overloaded calendar and sleepless nights. You who break the speed limit rushing to get to the other side of town. Slow down and get on track intrinsically—from the inside out." He is reminding all of us, ever so lovingly, that regardless of what may be happening around us—economic upheaval, violence, racism, and rumors of war—He is in control. Moreover, if we tap into His being—the very essence and nature of who He is—everything will fall into its proper place because He will be honored and exalted. He will not cease being. Still, I can't help but wonder how often we miss the reminders as well as the opportunities of Psalm 46:10.

In my duality as a pastor and professor, I admit that our constant on-the-go culture, I-need-to-be-me culture, concerns me. More often than not, I find myself in the role of giving advice and counsel. The most reflective thoughts I have usually come from sessions where life-altering decisions have been made because of one's bent towards doing instead of being. I've watched as people have chosen professions, marriage partners, and even business opportunities that had nothing to do with their being—core values, essence, and non-negotiables—but everything to do with what they hoped those choices would do for them. A lot of their decisions also seemed to be predicated by what "everyone else was doing" without consideration of or even a conscious dumbing down of who that person was called to be. In a day where social media "likes" can outweigh morals, it's important to understand where you stand in relation to the proverbial line in the sand.

If you are struggling with being and find yourself always doing, take some time to read and meditate on these verses of Scripture:

Rejoice in hope, be patient in tribulation, be constant in prayer. —Romans 12:12 (ESV)

I have told you this so that through me you may have peace. In the world you'll have trouble, but be courageous—I've overcome the world! —John 16:33 (ISV)

But they that wait upon the LORD shall renew their strength; they shall mount up with wings as eagles; they shall run, and not be weary; and they shall walk, and not faint. —Isaiah 40:31 (KJV)

And do not be conformed to this world, but be transformed by the renewing of your mind, so that you may prove what the will of God is, that which is good and acceptable and perfect. —Romans 12:2 (NASB)

chapter 2

CULTURE AND LEADERSHIP

ACCORDING TO THEORIST Raymond Williams, culture is one of the most difficult words to define. In his seminal work, Culture and Society (1958), he stated that culture is "a whole way of life." Historically, culture has always had three subtle yet distinct meanings. In this regard, culture is institutional as in an organization's protocols, practices, and principles. Culture is individual as in one's personal pedigree, perspectives, and preferences. Lastly, culture is interdependent as in the collective behavior, group consciousness, and common bonds of a group or people. The word culture derives from the Latin root of *cultus* which means "care." It has French connotations derived from *colere* which means "to till, tend, inhabit, or cultivate." Culture is also defined as the characteristics and knowledge of a particular group of people which encompass language, religion, cuisine, social habits, music, arts, and symbols.

The Center for Advanced Research on Language Acquisition defines culture as "shared patterns of behaviors and interactions, cognitive constructs, and affective understanding that are learned by socialization." Ken Myers, host of Mars Hill Audio Journal, asserts that "Human cultures are more complex, since they also include beliefs, ideas, and the spiritual aspects of human personhood. But those intangible elements are only sustained by taking form. Cultures may be said to be inherently incarnational, the spirit necessarily taking flesh for a culture to be present (Myers, Ken. [2016]. "What Is Culture?" *www.thegospelcoalition.com*)." In this regard, culture is both spirit and truth as it incorporates every area of life, personhood, and existence.

I asked two sisters in the faith Mercy Lokulutu, a registered nurse, ordained pastor, and author and Karrianna Turner, pastor of Emerging Generations at New Birth Baptist Church and social media influencer, to share their thoughts on culture. Mercy said,

> Culture to me is a worldview and outlook that both outlines and fulfills your vision, mission and values. In a personal space, the expression of my culture is heavily influenced by the country I was born in, Nigeria, as well as experiences in my young adult years. I will readily admit that my personal cultural, ideals, and moral worldview have shifted in my late adult years, and I shape it using the Bible as my principal ethos and resourcing myself with tools to improve my leadership skills. In the workplace, I use the company culture as a broad guideline to help make the mission and vision become practical and tangible. —@mercylokulutu (IG)

Karri added,

> Craig Groeschel expressed "Your culture is a combination of what you create and what you allow." I personally love his sentiments, as it makes it very apparent that culture is

not some mysterious entity that merely falls out of the sky, however, culture is wrapped in responsibility and account-ability by everyone engaged within any communal context where culture is being established and cultivated. Culture is fostered by the decisions and actions I take each day as a leader. It is the intentional design of the cultural climate promoted within in the community in which I serve. It is how I lead, love, embrace and honor others as I honor God. Culture is engaging the hearts, ideas and thoughts of those I lead by creating a safe, open, honest and loving at-mosphere to do so. Culture is also what I consent to as a leader. It is what I deem acceptable for myself and those in which I lead. Developing and encouraging culture is what I believe to be a beautiful, yet challenging dance of taking responsibility for my leadership in modeling culture, while also nurturing mutual accountability with amongst those I have the privilege of leading to ensure that we all are doing our very best to maintain the culture and community in which we passionately and collectively believe in through our thoughts and deeds. —@mzkarribaby (IG)

UNIVERSAL UNDERSTANDING OF CULTURE

As shared, culture is a difficult term to define as it means different things and connotes different nuances to different people. For our purposes, we will rely heavily on the definition of culture provided by Gudykunst and Ting-Toomey (1988) who define culture as "the way of life, customs, and script of a group of people." We will also consider Dutch psychologist Geert Hofstede who believes that culture is how we understand unwritten rules about how to be a good member of society (*geerthofstede.com/culture-geert-hofstede-gert-jan-hofstede/6d-model-of-national-culture/*). His pioneering work, a cultural dimensions model, is a globally recognized tool used to understand cultural differences: The 6–D Model of International Culture.

The six components of the model are as follows:

1. **Power Distance Index (high versus low):** The PDI describes the amount of inequality that exists in a culture and is accepted.
2. **Individualism vs. Collectivism:** The IDV defines the connections people have to their communities.
3. **Masculinity vs. Femininity:** The MAS refers to the assignment of gender roles and norms to men and women.
4. **Uncertainty Avoidance Index (high versus low):** The UAI measures how well people cope with pressure, stress, and anxiety.
5. **Long-Versus Short-Term Orientation:** This dimension categorizes a nation's focus based on its outlook over time and its expectations.
6. **Indulgence vs. Restraint:** The IVR relates how countries view individual self-indulgence as opposed to self-control.

The power and beauty of the 6-D Model of International Culture is that it provides a broad yet targeted approach to how people in different cultures observe, think and behave. It also measures the impact of cultural norms on interpersonal behavior. I am fond of the 6-D Model because it provides a roadmap regarding how to adjust one's behavior to be more acceptable in terms of cultural norms when entering into established, new, or foreign environments.

In effect, culture connects and intersects. Culture includes what you say and how you say it. Culture influences what you wear, how and why you wear it. Culture dictates what you eat, when and where you eat it. Culture also impacts what you speak, when and where you speak it and what you believe and why you believe it. However, for different people, culture means different things.

I asked Dina Marto, an entrepreneur, music executive, and founder of Twelve Music Group, to detail what culture means to her. She shared,

> Recently, I think the word "culture" has become trendy and overused. To me, it means the authentic tone, vibe, and ideals of a particular group or location. Therefore, the culture changes depending on different situations. As a music executive and entrepreneur, I do not dictate the culture of Hip-Hop. I help support and grow the talent and artistry of the people within the culture. I help create business opportunities for creatives in which they are able to showcase and speak for the often voiceless and misunderstood. This is how I help lead—by not imposing my personal opinions, but by guiding my clients and allowing them to flourish and tell their own stories.

Separately, as an Arab American woman, I am constantly balancing the traditions of my upbringing along with the society in which I live. My roots and strong family foundation give me the ability to walk in different worlds and still appreciate my principles while being able to celebrate and be a part of other cultures. I believe we need more of this openness—to realize we are more similar than we are different and not allow the dynamic of these differences to limit our own universe. —@DinaMarto (IG)

As Dina's experiences detail, doing something for one's culture can mean one thing publicly and an entirely different thing privately as many cultural influencers and taste-makers represent a multiplicity of interwoven and even diverse—yet complimentary—socio, economic, racial, gender, and religious compounded interests.

CULTURE AND LEADERSHIP

Let's begin by stating the obvious. One of the primary purposes and intersectional pulls of leadership is to create culture. By way of review, culture is a set of beliefs about how we think, what we believe, what we value, and how we create and influence the environments around us. Similarly, leadership is a mechanism of influence used to motivate, equip, and empower others positively to the achievement of a goal or outcome. For me, leadership is also a trifecta of influence, mission, and vision (common goals) aligned within a group of people willing to journey towards positive transformative change. My definition of leadership speaks to what experts in the field have written about this subject. In particular, leadership guru John Maxwell states, "Leadership is influence—nothing more, nothing less." In this regard, leadership can also be seen as "a process of social influence which maximizes the efforts of others towards the achievement of a goal." I believe Warren Bennis said it best: "Leadership is the capacity to translate vision into reality."

One of the most critical ingredients needed to turn said vision into reality is influence in that it gives one the ability to guide others towards a particular end. Peter Drucker suggests, "Leadership is the lifting of a man's vision to higher sights, the raising of a man's performance to a higher standard, the building of a man's personality beyond its normal limitations." And, Bill Gates advocates that effective leadership empowers others. Combined, leadership and culture organize the thoughts, feelings, values, and outcomes of people, leaders, institutions, communities, and organizations.

Historically, the notion of empowering others has been counterintuitive to traditional models of leadership which focused on hierarchical and patriarchal models of male dominance. In teaching millennials, they've profusely expressed that leadership models that speak to the inherent dominance of one group of people over another are off-putting. Three traditional models of leadership—the Great Man Theory, Trait Theory, and Management Theory—tend to illicit the most pushback from this highly collaborative, action-oriented, and cause-conscious collective. For millennials, more participation-oriented, lift-each-other-up-as-we-climb models of leadership such as Participative Leadership,

Transformative Leadership, and Authentic Leadership resonate. Each of these models has distinctive characteristics.

THE GREAT MAN THEORY OF LEADERSHIP

Perhaps the most well-known and globally recognized model of leadership is the great man theory. Popularized in the 19th century by historian Thomas Carlyle, the theory asserts that leadership is an inherent trait endowed to a certain group of men. They possess extraordinary abilities to impact the world and make change. These "great" leaders are said to be born with certain traits or qualities that cause them to stand out especially in times of crisis and/or conflict. According to Carlyle, "The history of the world is but the biography of great men."

THE TRAIT THEORY OF LEADERSHIP

The trait theory of leadership was also established in the 19th century, and some also credit Carlyle with its early foundation. The theory posits that certain people possess inherent qualities and skills that predispose them to successful leadership. These traits usually come from a variety of psychological, behavioral, intellectual, and even physiological domains which combine to make some people more suited for leadership than others.

SKILLS THEORY OF LEADERSHIP

The skills theory of leadership examines the types of abilities or assets leaders possess and how those abilities help them lead effectively. An obvious remix of trait theory, the skill approach was introduced in 1955 through the research of Robert Katz. In his analysis, Katz observed three dominant skills that executives relied on in leading organizations. These skills were grouped into three distinct categories: technical, human, and conceptual.

SITUATIONAL THEORY OF LEADERSHIP

The situational theory of leadership was developed by Hershey and Blanchard, and as the name implies, suggests that there are a variety of leadership styles that can be utilized, depending on the situation. In effect, to be seen as a good situational leader, one must be able and willing to adapt one's leadership style to meet both the needs of the people as well as deal with what is happening at any given moment.

BEHAVIORAL THEORY OF LEADERSHIP

The behavioral theory focuses on the development of leaders through an examination of their actions. In addition, it attempts to equip them to develop behaviors that are conducive to leading groups and teams. In effect, the behavioral model—in that it suggests that leadership can be taught and/or conditioned—refutes the great man theory. Researchers of this model classified leadership behavior into two realms: task behaviors and relationship behaviors.

DEMOCRATIC THEORY OF LEADERSHIP

The democratic theory encourages all group and team members to participate in the decision-making and leadership processes.

Also known as participative management, it welcomes the free exchange of concepts and ideas and is in direct opposition to top-down, bureaucratic models of control. The democratic model focuses on the collective consciousness of the group while reserving the right of the leader to operate as a coach and make the final decision for or issue the final directive to the team.

MANAGEMENT THEORY OF LEADERSHIP

The management or transactional theory focuses on supervision and performance within an organization. The pioneer of this school of thought, German sociologist Max Weber, engaged in an extensive study of leadership styles and developed the rational-legal authority—also known as the bureaucratic model of leadership. It is one of the most traditional models of leadership in that it is a top-down model that focuses on the exchange that happens between leaders and his or her followers.

TRANSFORMATIONAL THEORY OF LEADERSHIP

The transformational theory is a model of leadership that focuses on the measurable improvement of people, groups, and organizations by concentrating on values, standards, goals, and long-term added value. Transformative leaders do this primarily by shifting organizational atmospheres away from self-interested and self-preserving entities to cause-driven collective communities attentive to the greater good. In effect, organizations and people go from being "me" centered to mission-driven and others-centered. These noticeably drastic yet healthy organizational and leadership changes tend to be orchestrated by highly charismatic, inspirational, and visionary leaders who are missional in focus and in appeal.

AUTHENTIC LEADERSHIP

Authentic leadership is a management and leadership style rooted and grounded in honesty, transparency, and self-awareness. According to Fred O. Walumbwa and his colleagues, authentic leadership is a "pattern of leader behavior that draws upon and promotes both positive psychological capacities and a positive ethical climate, to foster greater self-awareness, an internalized moral perspective, balanced processing of information, and relational transparency on the part of leaders working with followers, fostering positive self-esteem."

SERVANT–LEADERSHIP

One of the newest models of leadership, Robert Greenleaf first introduced this concept in the 1970s in an essay he wrote on the transformative power of leading by serving others first. According to this theory, 10 characteristics shape servant leaders: listening, empathy, healing, awareness, persuasion, conceptualization, foresight, stewardship, commitment to others, and building community.

A CASE STUDY—BE THE ANSWER

One of the earliest and fondest memories I have of my husband, Mo, whom I still admire to this day, is the way he takes ownership of things and is a great steward of the environments he finds himself in. He epitomizes servant leadership. It doesn't matter where we find ourselves—at church, in a movie theater, on a walk—whenever he sees something that needs to be done, he does it. Whether it is personally picking up trash from the church parking lot or getting a napkin to clean popcorn out of a chair, he always takes initiative to remedy a situation.

I remember when I asked him why he makes it a point to be the answer time and time again. His answer was simple. He said, "I always want to be someone who takes ownership to make things better. I want to be a good steward of every environment or person I encounter. I want to add value. I want to help." In over a decade of dating and marriage, I can tell you his servant-leader heart is stilling beating—and being—the answer. He even wrote a book about it: *Be The Answer*. Recently, while on staycation, we visited our local park, and Mo did what he always does. Two boys were playing catch with a football, and one of the boys knocked one of the chairs in the park over. Before we left, I watched as my husband went over to the area of the downed chair. He asked the young guy his name and picked up the chair before we walked home. In all things and in all ways, we have the opportunity to be the answer and change—not just maintain—the status quo in our environments.

chapter 3

FOR THE CULTURE?

A S QUIET AS it is kept, overlooked, and even ignored, there is the obvious and inevitable reality of culture. It changes. Absolutely, unequivocally, and even predictably, culture will and must change. Psychologists and anthropologists alike agree that it's a part of its evolutionary make-up and a necessity for its regeneration. No matter what culture people are a part of, one thing is for certain, it will change.

One explanation for the dynamic nature of culture change is offered by anthropologist Christina De Rossi. In writing about the proximity of people, places, and things, De Rossi noted that "culture appears to have become key in our interconnected world, which is made up of so many ethnically diverse societies, but also riddled by conflicts associated with religion, ethnicity, ethical beliefs, and, essentially, the elements which make up culture." She added, "Culture is no longer fixed, if it ever was. It is essentially fluid and constantly in motion."

I agree with her assessment. I also believe that whenever we define culture in a particular way or make broad strokes of what culture is without taking into consideration its evolutionary and historic dimensions of change, we fail. Culture is supposed to be an articulator. However, devoid of change, often it becomes an artifact. In this regard, I believe it is critical to examine the constancy of change in culture because it's a game changer. Think about it. How many times have we heard, been subject to, or even been an advocate or proponent of culture that didn't take into account the historical as well as modern-day realities of culture change? How many times have we been influenced or overtaken by culture change that is "all the rage"? Today, it's TicTok. Who knows what it will be next month? No matter the process, we've ALL gone through the excitement and growth pains of change.

HASHTAG CULTURE

One of the most interesting happenings we all find ourselves a part of are #culture movements. While seemingly arbitrary and reactive, these largely social media phenomena have a way of polarizing the most united houses of faith. Galvanizing around common causes, they use their collective voice to inject social consciousness and social justice advocacy into a variety of economic, racial, social, and political "hot-button" topics and issues. Most uniquely, they have been able to inject truth to power demands as well as expectations into the national and international thought space through a like, retweet, or click. In particular, many of the hashtag movements while visibly and audibly visceral, have been responsible for bringing global attention and awareness to long-standing institutional issues that have been ignored or swept under the rug for centuries.

Two of the most interesting hashtag movements that have completely piqued my interest are the #cancelculture and #fortheculture movements. Both of these largely social media phenomena have over 1 million hashtags and have sparked unprecedented dialogue, debate, discussion, and, in a few instances, transformative change. If I can be completely honest, before I ever did any in-depth research or study on these two movements, I was already captivated because of the use of what I think is one of the most effective disarming tools—humor. Yes, you've got it right. I remember the very first time I came upon a cancel culture gif. I lol'd, rotflmbo'd, and smh'd. The year was 2015, and this soon-to-be-known tsunami of twitter fingers also known as "Black Twitter" began to use its collective power and online social capital to call out, challenge, and even demand the cancellation of people, places, events, and statements its "police" deemed culturally insensitive, ignorant, inappropriate, and even appropriated.

To be factually accurate, however, in a 2019 *Vox* article, Aja Romano dates the first appearance of cancel culture to the 2001 film New Jack City when the main protagonist Nino Brown numbly canceled his girlfriend. In 2010, rapper Lil Wayne reintroduced the phrase by referencing the aforementioned larger-than-life film. Fast-forward to the beginning of 2015. Cancel culture went from being used as lighthearted humor to disagree with someone who didn't like what you liked—for example, "You didn't grow up watching 'Martin'?" #canceled—to a full-blown social media and larger-societal tool. Used to call out those in positions of power especially in the sports, entertainment, and political arenas considered to engage in culturally insensitive and inappropriate behavior, cancel culture has taken on a life of its own.

Interestingly, linguistics professor Anne Charity Hudley, who was referenced in the same *Vox* article, likened the cancel culture movement to the Civil Rights boycotts of the 1950s and 1960s. She stated,

> Canceling is a way to acknowledge that you don't have the power to change structural inequality... When you see people canceling Kanye, canceling other people, it's a collective way of saying, "We elevated your social status, your economic prowess, [and] we're not going to pay attention to you in the way that we once did …. I may have no power, but the power I do have is to [ignore] you."

Similar yet different in its call for collective group consciousness and action is the #fortheculture movement which promotes black success, magic, joy, empowerment, unity, and solidarity. Some of its most viral hashtags are #blackgirlmagic and #blackboyjoy. Both hashtags were designed to shine light and bring attention to all of the buoyancy, brilliance, and brightness within the African American culture. When someone says #blackgirlmagic or #blackboyjoy it's meant to connote racial accomplishment, success, and pride in spite of the systematic, institutional, and legal barriers still present to prevent the fullness of the Founding Fathers' declaration that all "men" are "endowed by their Creator with certain unalienable Rights. Among these are the rights to life, liberty, and property."

Although Jay Z said, "I do it for my culture," in the early 2000s, the term really took off and was widely received in the urban vernacular through Atlanta hip-hop trio the Migos, circa 2017. In a song called "T-Shirt," rapper Quavo spits (raps), "Do it for the culture, They gon bite like vultures." Essentially, do it for the culture is a collective call to positive action to utilize the social capital and economic spending power of everyday black people, leaders, and celebrities to elevate—not denigrate—the positive and progressive steps within black, urban, and youth cultures.

Doing it for the culture, in effect, is personal acknowledgment and ownership of black and brown social, political, racial, and economic power and uplift as black actors, rappers, and athletes use their global platforms to bring awareness and resources to issues that have often been maligned or ignored. Case in point, the attention given to the senseless and brutal deaths of Ahmaud Arbery, Breonna Taylor, George Floyd, and most recently Elijah McClain—in large measure—came as a result of celebrities, politicians, and Christian influencers and leaders using their platforms and voices to speak out and demand action and justice on behalf of these lost African American lives.

While I wholeheartedly agree with both of these movements in theory, I'm not always sure about the long term affect and effect of canceling living beings. Moreover, if as the 6-D Model indicates, culture means different things to different people groups, how can we truly cancel culture or do it for the culture. In effect, when we attempt to cancel culture, we may ignore the subcultures, hidden cultures, and yet-to-be-developed cultures within the larger culture. Similarly, when we do it for the culture, do we give room for those who are not biologically or genetically a part of the culture to speak up and/or advocate on behalf of the culture? The point, quite simply, is that no one truly has monolithic power to do it for the culture or cancel culture.

I asked Pastor Jonathan "YPJ" Miller to give me his take on it. He shared,

> I believe we need to cancel cancel culture. It is a merciless and emotionally driven practice that in most cases does not have sound validity behind its demonstration. Whereas there are some things that need to be eliminated from culture, most incidents where a person errs are not beyond reconciliation or restoration. If we cancel people, we sow a seed that we ourselves will reap a harvest of, thus creating an unnecessary pressure for us to uphold a standard of perfection that we can't keep. We need a mercy—not a cancel—culture.
> —@PastorYPJ (IG)

While profoundly true, we obviously aren't there yet. At best, we are in a #calloutculture as was the case with Pastor Chris Hodges and his screen-grabbed series of likes in support of President Trump.

MERCILESS CULTURE

"And some of us who have already begun to break the silence of the night have found that the calling to speak is often a vocation of agony, but we must speak. We must speak with all the humility that is appropriate to our limited vision, but we must speak." —"A Time to Break Silence," Dr. Martin L. King, Jr.

Rapper Lecrae and Pastor Louie Giglio have also been subjected to what now has arguably morphed into a merciless culture. The calls to punitively cancel both leaders occurred when Giglio stated, "...But we miss the blessing of slavery, that it actually built up the framework for the world that white people live in and lived in," during a conversation on race at Passion City Church. Both Giglio and Lecrae issued public statements of explanation and even social media apologies—one for attempting to put a positive spin on a painful historical and current reality and the other explaining why he remained silent in response. In spite of the quick public address from both, the 2-minute clip went viral with both the sacred and the secular culture going ham on (using extraordinary and even aggressive effort against) the two leaders. The absence of mercy for either leader or the debacle that ensued, to me, speaks to what can only classified as the ill-natured effect of mob culture. Let's be clear: The clip is all bad all around. However, when efforts are made to acknowledge missteps and teachable moments are still met with crowd chants of "Cancel Them" we have a problem with the rate and pace of change in our culture.

The reality of the indiscriminate nature of today's cancel and call-out culture is that if he were alive today, I believe even Dr. King could be subject to a merciless cancel-culture mentality. As such, it's important that we tell truth in love, speak truth to power, and per Micah 6:8 (NIV) "act justly, to love mercy and to walk humbly with [our] God." In doing this, we can guard against cancel, call-out, consumer, and even no-response culture—all of which limit us from rediscovering lost values and inhibit us from being as leaders.

chapter 4

YOU ARE A CULTURE OF ONE

I N   T H E   L A S T chapter, we spent time detailing some of the history of culture. Given the magnitude of its scope and reach, I think it's fair to say that culture isn't just a way of life, culture is life! It is all around us. It organizes us. It points, clicks, and directs us. It precedes us. It leads us. It can even deceive us. Still, it is a mainstay that dictates and often influences the values, beliefs, and behaviors that shape us. With such a loud and pronounced global footprint, culture can seem like it's all-consuming. The truth of the matter is that culture—as powerful and pervasive as it is—shouldn't dominate us as much as it should be influenced, informed, created, and shaped by us. Personally, I think culture should operate similar to the philosophy of the '90s clothing brand FUBU (For Us By Us). The brand, started by four young African American entrepreneurs and friends, was designed to "make clothing for the consumer by the consumer." As you can imagine, the brand skyrocketed to success because the consumers of the culture took responsibility and began to create the culture. Until consumers of culture become creators of culture, we will forever be dictated to by culture. As such, I believe now, more than even, there is a need around the world for a new breed of disruptors and innovators of culture.

CULTURE OF ONE

Oftentimes we relegate the word "one" to its surface-level meaning of being a part of a numerical counting system or being the first in an order or pairing. While these ideas are factual, one also means to be a member of a group, to be a single ordering of a thing, or to be one in particular. According to Strong's Concordance, one in Greek is *sozo* (Strong's Number 4982) which is translated in the New Testament as "safe" or "rescued" as in salvation, whole, healed, or to keep safe and sound. A deeper dive into its word usage indicates that one also means being the same in kind or quality, the number denoting unity, at harmony, in agreement, and whole. It is within this framework that I want to examine the word. I want to look at one through the lens of being complete, whole, congruent, and lacking nothing. To be a "culture of one" means you are an individual, and the beliefs, values, principles and practices that shape you are integrated, harmonious, in agreement, and aligned.

In essence, to the best of your ability, you operate in authenticity and congruency. In both head (thinking) and heart (feeling), you are one as it relates to what you believe and why you believe it, who and what you value and why you value them, what principles and practices you live by, and why you live by and reinforce those principles and practices in your family, friendships, leadership, organizations, institutions, and spheres of influence. More importantly, as a leader, you are a culture of one because you set the tone, pace, and environment of the culture.

No matter how big or small your audience and environment, those who work and serve alongside you are given both verbal and nonverbal culture cues based on what you say and do. *Selah*, and let that "sizzle in your spirit" as comedian Kountry Wayne likes to say. Let me say it again for those reading this while riding your Peloton. THOSE WHO WORK ALONGSIDE YOU ARE GIVEN BOTH VEBAL AND NONVERBAL CULTURE CUES BASED ON WHAT YOU SAY AND DO! I know this may be a bit difficult to swallow as you may wonder, How do my nonverbal cues impact culture? As a leader, ask yourself, "Am I intentional about saying, 'Hello,' to every person I encounter on my way to the office?" In practical terms, do you know how many people, on average, you will have an opportunity to impart organizational culture to on your way to your workspace? Think about it! From the time you exit your vehicle until you enter your office, you probably pass security and staff in the parking lots and hallways. You may even encounter your direct report.

If you don't do so already, try saying, "Hello," waving, or doing something to acknowledge the presence and the humanity of those individuals you pass along the way. To be clear, I understand that time is usually tight, and you aren't just coming into the office to twiddle your thumbs and do nothing. However, I also understand what Brené Brown says when she states, "Clear is kind." I say it this way: If clarity is kindness, being present in the moment produces the leadership gold of mindfulness.

As leaders, we have to be transparent. Our intentions, motives, and ways of being and thinking must be well-defined. In choosing to speak to those you're passing—on your way to where you are going—I believe you clarify the obvious and state through your actions, "I SEE YOU" which is the longing of every human soul. In leadership and life, "I SEE YOU" in verbal acknowledgment goes a long way on the highway of social capital and emotional intelligence.

I asked my friend Summer Bowie, Assistant Senior Pastor of Victory Church, how she tries to create culture. She shared,

Culture is the imprint I leave with people through [the] expressed values, beliefs, and behaviors that I impart as a leader. It's the experience I extend to others in my everyday interactions as I live, as I move, and by just being with people. 3 things are at the forefront in shaping the environment where I lead. In a leadership culture, being as leading for me begins with a heart of humility that extends love to others, while providing a safe and caring environment for them to grow and be challenged.

HUMILITY

I believe that nobody is perfect, and not one person is better than another. As a leader, while I might have a greater organizational authority, that doesn't mean I think of myself better than anyone else, or place myself in an elite status. To be an effective leader, leadership begins with a heart of humility. It begins by me seeing others the way Christ sees them. It begins by valuing them and recognizing the talents God has placed in them while celebrating them for their accomplishments. And [it] says this isn't about me building an organization, it's about us working together for what God wants to do through the environments where we lead.

LOVE

Years ago, I was spending time with God and I read the scripture found in John 13:34-35. I do my best to live by it. As a Christ follower, who leads in the church, I want to represent the heart of Jesus in my leadership. I recognized—and still do to this day—that true leadership begins with a heart of humility while extending love to others. Before I was given the privilege of leading in the church, I became a disciple of Christ. So, I'm a disciple before I am a leader. One of the greatest ways we can extend love to others is by being present with them.

SAFETY AND CARE

There is the saying: "People don't care how much you know, until they know how much you care." I've found this to be true in leadership culture. When humility and love lead in a leadership culture, people feel valued, people feel safe, people feel cared for, and people will walk 1,000 miles with you. When these things are in place, a healthy leadership culture begins to grow, and reproduce in the areas that you lead. —@summerbowie1 (IG)

There are so many positive and transformative cultural cues we can give to those around us that don't cost us anything. Here are a few to consider:

1. Be the first to speak and acknowledge others.
2. Genuinely and authentically listen to others.
3. Be intentional in connecting with others.
4. Be intentional to not let your preferences dictate organizational culture.
5. Create safe spaces for others to voice their opinions and perspectives.
6. Avoid public and private shaming of others.
7. Honor those below you as well as you honor those above you.
8. Create a gossip-free culture.
9. Create a culture that is based on values—not uniformity.
10. Model what you want others to emulate in thought, word, deed, and action.

DISCLAIMER ALERT

Let me insert a personal disclaimer. I'm not offering these suggestions out of some sort of soapbox angst. I share as they're the leadership and culture cues I have to constantly work on and practice. Being a classic type A, Enneagram 5, task-oriented introvert who around the age of 12 had mastered delayed gratification and the notion of working hard now and playing later, I can get lost in my own thought sauce. Long story short, at times, I still don't slow down long enough to unearth the leadership gold around me. I can struggle with being still and knowing, or even being fully present when speaking to others because I'm consumed with my internal to-do list.

One time, I was approached by a campus safety officer who worked at my university. I was exiting a local bank as he was entering. I remember this older and wise-looking man ask if he could share something with me. Intrinsically, I cringed because the internal stopwatch by which I dictated my life didn't have time for this unplanned interruption. Grudgingly, I complied, and what happened next put me on the needed path and trajectory to leadership gold aka mindfulness.

He shared that more often than I know he has observed me coming and going around campus. He asked if he could offer two suggestions. "First," he said, "please slow down." He said, "I noticed you always seem to be in a rush and rapidly moving from one place to the next—slow down and take in all that life has to offer." The second thing he shared was this observation: "You always seem to walk with your head down. I guess you're thinking. Young lady, I'm former military, and I want to encourage you to walk with your head up and smile." I think somewhere etched along the walls of church canon, along with that church mother outfit, are the words "If you can't say 'Amen,' say 'Ouch.'" On that day, I had to say amen to the words of a relative stranger in English, Hebrew, and Greek. He had spoken the truth in love and challenged me to examine the bodily posture and actions of my culture of one.

Honestly, his words weren't easy to hear because while I knew I was always in a rush—preoccupied with getting from one classroom to another, one way, across campus, on time—I didn't consciously know that I walked with my head down. Further, while I was aware (still am) that my brain is on "go" and thinking all of the time, I didn't realize that it caused me to smile less. How ironic that I went to the bank to make a deposit but left the bank with even greater life and leadership dividends. To this day, I have to be mindful to not go back to my old and trusted introverted self of head-down, thinking-cap-on, mission-driven focus, devoid of being people-centered and present-in-the-moment centered. Some days it still feels uncomfortable to create new culture cues. However, if I want to create healthy culture especially in my culture of one, I must be both the creator as well as disruptor of even my own disabling culture.

READ AND LEAD YOUR CULTURE

First things first. Before you can be a shaper and leader of culture, you must be a reader and leader of your own personal culture. Why? As a leader you set the tone, pace, and environment of the culture. You must know this and own this if you are going to be a responsible shaper and steward of culture. Far too many leaders wonder why their organizational cultures are the way they are without taking an honest look at the ways in which their personal values, beliefs, and preferences have spilled over and sometimes contaminated organization culture and morale. How many of us know or have been subject to a leader who leads from a place of anger, control, or my-way-or-the-highway stubbornness? While it's a known fact that things get done within that organization, it is also a known fact that tensions are high, and some within the organization have their therapists on speed dial. Now let me be very clear: I am all for #Jesusandtherapy. What I am not for, however, are environments full of fear, condemnation, and angst. The problem is that many environments are highly managerial with transactional cultures where there is only one-to-one exchange of rewards and punishments.

I love how Christine Villano Ware, PulteGroup Inc., IT Business Relationship Manager, Construction and Customer Care, is changing the game and creating a culture-of-one leadership style infused with intentionality, consciousness, and care. She believes,

> Culture to me involves creating an environment of trust and safety within my team. As the leader it's my responsibility to create and develop the culture over time. There will always be the pressure of deadlines and unrealistic demands from our business stakeholders. I strive to never sacrifice the culture and health of my team because I'm afraid to say no or even worse, commit to a date prematurely and expect or demand my team to make it happen.
>
> If my ultimate goal is to create a culture of trust and safety, I need to understand the hearts of the individuals I serve. How do I do this? I meet with team members individually on a regular cadence. I'll schedule bi-weekly or monthly 1:1s, lunch or walk-by's to briefly chat or check in with my

folks individually. It's important for me to be present with those I serve. This means putting my phone away during 1:1s and following through on action items assigned to me. I listen better when I'm present. I ask probing questions to further unpack a thought or an idea to make sure I understand the underlying message or perspective. I allow space in the conversation so team members feel more comfortable to share what is truly on their hearts—personally or professionally. I try to be intentional not to fix their problems but empower them to discover the solutions for themselves. I want my team to feel comfortable enough to share even if it's something I may not want to hear.

I speak words of encouragement when they become critical of themselves. When I notice toxic behavior, I do my best to address it quickly and privately. If I let bad behavior slide, I sacrifice the culture of our team. I aspire for our team to be best in class in how we treat one another. To flourish individually and collectively to achieve a common goal. To allow my team to feel empowered to show up every day and do their best work. —@cjvillano (IG)

Failure to incorporate the voices and wisdom of others will lead to nothing more than a top-down, dictatorial, great man theory of leadership culture where opinions and opportunities are limited or blocked, and no one is allowed to take the lead. In order to avoid this fatal flaw in leadership, ask yourself the following questions, and honestly and transparently answer them:

1. Am I being the same when everyone is around vs. when no one is around?
2. Am I open to the feedback, opinions, and thoughts of those who don't think like me?
3. Do I have intrinsic beliefs about how things should be as opposed to being open to what things could be?
4. Do I believe my cultural heritage is superior or better than other cultures I'm leading?
5. Do I have a difficult time letting go of my preferences and leaning into other people's preferences?
6. Do I give others permission to speak into my blind spots as a manager or leader?
7. Do I hire people with different personalities than me?
8. Do I exercise and engage in empathy and vulnerability with my team?
9. Do I make efforts to connect with others on my team outside of "the work"?
10. Do I celebrate small wins with those I lead?
11. One of the most effective ways to hold yourself accountable is to build a team of strong leaders around you where leadership and culture are built in consultation and in the multitude of council.

H.E.A.R.T.

One of the most important aspects of your leadership is your heart. Your heart determines everything about how you lead, for it is the storehouse of your leadership thinking and wiring.

If you are going to be an effective culture of one, you may have to start off by wearing your heart on your proverbial sleeve. As a leader, especially leading organizations with culture drift or the absence of clarity of culture, you will have to go first and let your emotions be felt and seen. To wear your heart on your sleeve means to let it all hang out as it relates to your leadership passions, desires, fears, and trepidations. I know this can be a lot to ask of certain types of Myers-Briggs leaders. Don't blame me, blame Shakespeare. In his classic *Othello,* Iago lamented,

> It is as sure as you are Roderigo,
> Were I the Moor, I would not be Iago.
> In following him, I follow but myself;
> Heaven is my judge, not I for love and duty,
> But seeming so, for my peculiar end;
> For when my outward action doth demonstrate
> The native act and figure of my heart
> In complement extern, 'tis not long after
> But I will wear my heart upon my sleeve
> For daws to peck at. I am not what I am.
>
> —*Othello,* Act 1, Scene 1, 56–65

These words command me to ask a question: When was the last time you led from a place where people could easily read you because your heart was so exposed and transparent people couldn't help but be compelled to follow you as you follow Christ?

I ask as I remember some years back when Holy Spirit gently whispered in my ear about the power of heart while I was prepping to do a leadership training with Mo in Cape Town, South

Africa. Our company, Momon Leadership, had been invited to present a 3-hour training for a church network with campus sites all around the country. As I quietly sat and watched waves crashing onto the shore, God began to illuminate the depths of all the richness that is hidden in plain sight within the word heart. This seemingly overused and undervalued word is power-packed. Clearly, it was my time to see it for the fullness that it was and would continue to be for me and the others I've been blessed to share its meaning with. So, heeding instructions, I grabbed a blank sheet of paper. I invite you to do the same. With some space between your letters, write out the word HEART. Now take a moment to look at your sheet of paper and think about what you see within the word HEART. As I did this, I saw and heard two things. The first thing I saw was the word EAR. The second was the word HEAR. Mind blown. Tears flowing. I was like, OMG, why had I never seen this before? Praise break ensued. Just as I was about to break out in the electric slide, Holy Spirit gently prompted that there was more. As I gathered myself, I heard this: "You have to have an EAR to HEAR the HEART of those around you!" I then began to take the word HEART and connect the spaces in between the letters, and it's interesting how similar in shape both the ear and heart happen to be.

Being a leader who has an ear to hear the heart of another is a culture game changer. It speaks without speaking and creates emotional and social capital that goes beyond the moment to create organizational and leadership gold and culture change. Thinking back to the onset of COVID-19, I remember how Pastor Johnson Bowie, Senior Pastor of Victory Church, sensed the Lord speaking to him that Victory needed to move to a clearly established Sabbath for the entire church organization. He shared his heart that he believed a Friday sabbath across the board—all ministries, all departments, all campuses—needed to be implemented to honor the Lord and the staff. He also sensed that a day of rest to prioritize our faith in God and the health of our families was essential to creating a healthy church. While the entire team agreed that an established Sabbath was needed, there was genuine concern that we execute it in a way that was first of all honoring (It would require everyone to lean in.) and secondly, still able to provide quality ministry and care for our close to 20,000-member congregation.

A few days later, via Zoom, Pastor Johnson took a huge leap of faith and announced our Friday sabbath to the entire staff. The response, as you can imagine, was #priceless! The announcement was met with overwhelmingly positive cheers, chat comments, and even a few tears. To this day, the Friday sabbath has been a game changer for everyone at the church. It not only communicated our leader's heart to the staff but also that our leader had an ear to hear the hearts of God and his team.

WHERE DO YOU GROW FROM HERE?

Wherever you find yourself, whether alone or in a crowd, you are always a culture of one. Before social media, political pundits, popular podcasts, or pop culture impacts and influences you, you should influence those around you. Let's see how you can be a culture of one in your environment, thoughts, friendship circles, and legacy.

ENVIRONMENT

The beauty of being a culture of one is that you also get to shape and rethink your culture based on your own growth, evolution, and needs. Your environment is anywhere you set the dominant tone, pace, and atmosphere. It can be your home, your office/cubicle, your car, even your ears via your Airpods. By environment, I am also referring to your atmosphere, your personal space, your Zen zone, your decompression area, your creative place, and your safe haven. In a world seemingly out of anyone but God's control, it is important to create and protect space where you can be at one with your thoughts, views, values, and beliefs. In your environment, you should be clear about your expectations, requirements, boundaries, likes, and dislikes. The culture you create should reflect the values and beliefs you respect. For example, if you respect organization, your home should reflect such.

The challenge with being a culture of one is that you are also responsible for who and what you allow into your environment. If you respect and value work/life balance, but you constantly find yourself responding to calls and answering texts after established work hours, your environment will be off. As you can imagine, the challenge is that you have the sole responsibility of maintaining your culture of one. As such, you either have to exercise self-control or develop a strong accountability system to help you establish or maintain guard rails to keep your environment in alignment. You should be aware of your unique wiring as you attend to this:

1. Be aware of what brings you peace.
2. Be aware of what brings you stress.
3. Be aware of what you read, listen to, and watch.
4. Be aware of your needs.
5. Be aware of what adds value to you.
6. Be aware of what drains you.
7. Be aware of what triggers you.
8. Be aware of when you need to rest.
9. Be aware of what you need to do to decompress.
10. Be aware of what you do when you are at your best.

In being conscious of these things, you ultimately are dialing in to what makes and shapes your culture as well as what does and does not work for you and the culture you are called to create.

THOUGHTS

One of the most important places to maintain a positive, healthy, and godly culture of one is in our thoughts. While we all know this to be true, how many times have we allowed negative thoughts or speech to creep into our hearts, minds, and thought processes? How many times have we let the negative opinions and even criticisms of others shape us in a detrimental way? If we are going to be a culture of one in our thoughts, we have to stop negative words, thoughts, beliefs, and actions in their tracks. We have to be mindful of what we let in, and we have to feed ourselves positive thoughts and starve negative thoughts. A few practical things we can do to reinforce a culture of one in our thoughts are to read the Word of God to refresh and renew our minds. Listen to life-giving music, podcasts, and audio books. We can surround ourselves with positive and wise friends, mentors, and accountability partners. Develop a personal relationship with Holy Spirit and invite Him into your innermost thoughts. As you do this, consider these mercies:

1. Be careful with asking, "What's wrong with me?"
2. Be careful to not compare yourself to others.
3. Be careful to not overthink things.
4. Be careful to not overdramatize things.
5. Be careful to not turn into Chicken Little. (The sky is not falling!)
6. Be quick to forgive.
7. Be willing to start over.
8. Be willing to admit when you are wrong.
9. Be open to seeking professional help.
10. Be willing to have accountability partners in your life.

On your journey of being a culture of one in your thoughts, remember these admonitions:

Don't fake it because you won't make it: "For what shall it profit a man, if he shall gain the whole world, but lose his soul?" —Mark 8:36 (KJV)

Reveal it (whatever it is) so Jesus can heal it: "Casting all your care upon him; for he careth for you." —1 Peter 5:7 (KJV)

Perspective is everything: "In all thy getting get understanding." —Proverbs 4:7 (NKJV)

FRIENDSHIPS CIRCLES

You are also a culture of one in your friendship circles. In this regard, your values should always rise above and not be subject to compromise. You should be clear on your dos and don'ts as well as your non-negotiables. You should seek to build friendships and relationships based on mutual core values and not prestige, popularity, opportunities, or appearances. Also, be mindful of whom you call "Friend" as we are in an age where everyone is a "friend" thanks to Facebook. It's worth repeating that everyone can't and shouldn't be in the friend category. It's perfectly fine to categorize people as acquaintances, associates, colleagues, comrades, and friends. Let me be clear. While you don't have to stand on a soapbox with a megaphone in hand making public announcements about who is who in your life, it is perfectly fine to categorize people in your heart and mind.

I remember a mentor once saying that you shouldn't call anyone friend until you've really been through something. At first, it didn't make sense to me. Now it's crystal clear. The premise of the statement is that we need some type of litmus test to truly measure if a person can be one that sticks closer than a brother. Can your relationship be tried by the proverbial fire and come out on the other side solidified? If you aren't sure about this, and even if you just need some time to vet things out, don't be afraid to establish boundaries, standards, guard rails, expectations, and even parameters surrounding your associations and potential friendships.

A CASE STUDY—MY FRIEND JAMEELA

I am a born-again believer because my closest friend Jameela invited me to attend Allen A.M.E. Church the summer before we entered 6th grade. To be honest, I think it was all a divine set-up because the only thing I enjoyed about that sports camp was lunch. I usually ate by myself because I was both painfully shy and self-conscious, but one day during week three of camp, Jameela came up to me, along with her younger sister Aisha, introduced herself, and invited me to eat lunch with the two of them. I couldn't believe it! I said, "Yes!" faster than she could get the words out because I was so desirous of a friend that I could just be me with, and she allowed me to do just that. Fast-forward to the end of the summer. Jameela invited me to church. Wow, I thought. It wasn't just a summer-camp connection. I'll never forget that Sunday because everything was different than the Pentecostal church I usually attended with my nana—Lula Bell Logan. At Nana's church, everything was loud: the music, the preacher, the church mothers, and even the amens! Here, things were much quieter and orderly (Mind you, they stood up and sat down a lot.); although, Jameela seemingly left one major detail out.

The pastor of her church was this short, hip, and spunky woman named Reverend Deitra C. Bell. I was shook (in awe). I couldn't believe it. I had never seen a woman in such a powerful leadership role in the church. I leaned into the sermon and took notes until the end of the message when "Rev." as we affectionately called her did the salvation call. All of a sudden, my hands got sweaty. My throat got a lump in it, and my heart began to pound. I couldn't move because I was afraid to take that long walk to the front of the church and publicly confess Jesus as Lord and Savior.

I'd be lying to you if I told you the next Sunday I ran up to the altar. Nope. It took me several months, but like the good friend she was—and remains—Jameela walked with me. Our commitment and friendship to each other remains steadfast. From summer camp to salvation to the twists and turns of life which have included the death of my brother to the passing of her mom and most recently her miraculous healing from COVID-19 (She was on a ventilator for almost a week!), our friendship remains one of the most treasured gifts I've received this side of heaven.

LEGACY

Lastly, you are a culture of one in the legacy you create. What do you do now while you are still alive and present on the earth to impact people? What do people say about you when you aren't around? If —unbeknownst to you—a hidden camera crew were to follow you around and document your life, what would it record? For me, legacy is what we leave behind; it's the love, kindness, humility, compassion, and generosity we sow in the here and now.

One of the things I always say on the first day of a semester, especially in my Introduction to Leadership course, is that I hope that I share one nugget that can be a keepsake for life. I say this because in looking at the legacy of my mentors, leaders, and even loved ones who are no longer here on earth, the nuggets they shared with me are what have kept me going. One of my favorites that I keep close to my heart is from my nana. I had come home during winter break from my Ph.D. studies, and I had a lot on my mind trying to figure out my next steps as there was dissent amongst my dissertation committee about my research agenda. Sensing and feeling my heaviness, Nana looked me dead in the eyes and said this: "Ken-A-Pooh, stop thinking and start thanking God!"

Yes, Nana called me Pooh as my favorite childhood character was Winnie the Pooh. Those words: pointed—powerful—perspective-giving. To this day, when I'm overwhelmed, burdened, not quite sure what to do, I remember the life and legacy of Mrs. Lula Bell Logan, and I command my mind to stop thinking, and I command my spirit to start thanking God.

chapter 5

BE A CULTURAL ANTHROPOLOGIST

BY NOW, I think you have a clear understanding of and commitment to the journey of being as leading. It is in our being that we have freedom to lead from the seat of authority and unique wiring that God has handcrafted specifically in you and me. It is also in our being that as leaders we become more effective creators, shapers, and cultivators. In my opinion, there are many benefits to being this type of hands-on curator of culture. I believe one of the most remarkable ones is that you get to unearth the leadership gold of the people, practices, and principles within your organizational networks. In this chapter, we explore being as leading from the perspective of a cultural anthropologist. Let's journey together as we unearth the treasures in us and all around us.

First, let's establish a few things about the field of anthropology. Anthropology is the study of humanity. Specifically, it's the study of humans and how they organize the societies in which they live. Yet, it's also a merging of two fields of thought—anatomy and psychology—and that merging's affect of and effect on human beings and society past, present, and future. Essentially, anthropology is the study of human beings and culture. The people who make sense of these findings are anthropologists. Anthropologists study people and all things related to the intersectionality of culture, science, and humanity. Anthropologists are also seen as those who possess keen understanding of culture and society. They are bridge builders as they connect both natural science (biology) to the humanities (art and culture).

The study of anthropology can be traced back to 400 BC, and Herodotus is credited by most as its father and first thinker to document the patterns, thoughts, customs, and beliefs found throughout different cultures. There are four primary subfields of anthropology: archaeology, linguistics, physical anthropology, and cultural anthropology. *Sapien.com* details the nuance:

> Anthropologists use these and other approaches to study all aspects of human existence, past and present. We include in our numbers archaeologists, who study people (but not dinosaurs) from the material traces they leave; linguistic anthropologists, who understand humans from the ways they use language; and biological anthropologists and paleoanthropologists, who understand them from their long history and immense physical variety. We also include sociocultural anthropologists, who document the meanings humans

make of the different worlds they inhabit... given the circumstances in which they live.

In addition to the four main areas of study within the field, anthropologists also use a variety of data-collection methods to accomplish their research goals and agenda. Some of the most common and effective methods are as follows:

1. Participant Observation
2. In-depth Interviews
3. Focus Groups
4. Textual Analysis
5. Field Work
6. Modeling
7. Comparative Study

Whether individually or combined, these research methods have proven to be a staple wheelhouse within the discipline and have yielded both short-term as well as long-term results.

CULTURAL ANTHROPOLOGY

One of the specialized fields of study within the discipline of anthropology is cultural anthropology. Given Sir Edward Burnett Tylor's definition of culture as "that complex whole which includes knowledge, belief, art, morals, custom, and any other capabilities and habits acquired by man as a member of society," cultural anthropology is an essential area of study because of its focus on the intersectionality of people's beliefs, practices, and ways of life in society. Thus, cultural anthropology is the scientific study of humans and their cultural, social, biological, and environmental aspects of life. The field examines the symbiotic nature, role, and influence of society (established systems, norms, rules, and regulations) and the impact of how people in a collective societal system share, shape, and organize the world around them.

Cultural anthropology looks to find both patterns and variance in society and societal norms through observation, interaction, interviews, and the use of scientific measurement instruments such as surveys—past and the present. Using a triangulation of methods including but not limited to archeology, ethnography, and linguistics, a cultural anthropologist immerses him or herself into the culture by living and dwelling among those he or she is seeking to study to examine as well as excavate the similarities and differences among the identified people group. I believe that in order to be effective cultural anthropologists, we have to study the language, traditions, customs, and behaviors within our organizations, groups, and circles.

Margaret Mead was one of the most well-known modern cultural anthropologists. An outspoken voice on a variety of hot-button cultural issues, she was affectionately known as the "Mother to the World." Mead's research focused on gender and racial differences, the environment, population control, and sexuality. She is most famously known for saying, "Never doubt that a small group of thoughtful, committed citizens can change the world: Indeed, it's the only thing that ever has." If I could lift this quote and apply it to our lens of analysis, I'd offer this revision: Never doubt how your presence, passion, and purpose—together—work to produce a vibrant and healthy culture where people know they can develop and grow from established core values that eliminate competition, favoritism, or greed in the workplace.

RIDING SHOTGUN

I believe it's supremely important to become a cultural anthropologist within the environment you serve and lead because you need to have a first-hand, up-close opportunity to inspect what you expect. In doing so, you have an opportunity to retool and reimagine, eliminate any mindsets or mentalities that are opposed to your mission and outcomes, and even restore or remove artifacts (people, policies, or ways of doing things) that are no longer healthy or effective in creating or sustaining a replicative environment. Recall, it is also Margaret Mead who said, "What people say, what people do, and what they say they do are entirely different things." We can say all day every day that we want to inspect what we expect in our environments. However, until we call shotgun and take a ride around our organizational cultures, we won't be able to implement change or foster environments of purposive praise in our leadership culture.

In taking on the mantle of being cultural anthropologists in our organizations, we communicate our willingness to do two things. We go first and are connoisseurs as well as critics of the culture we think others ought to consume. And, we communicate our commitment to change.

LET'S DIG

Earlier in the chapter, I mentioned that one of the most beautiful things about being as leading from the lens of a cultural anthropologist is that you get to unearth the gold and hidden treasures within yourself and others. While the end result of this dig is priceless, I want to establish a disclaimer on the front end. There are times when going on an archaeological dig can be time-consuming, expensive, and even messy. It's a painstaking process that requires patience and self-discipline. There can be early mornings and long nights with no seeming end in sight. While a dig's opportunity costs and even life-altering discoveries can be monumental, there remain both the known and unknown risks of loss, failure, and even death.

At best, embarking upon a dig to excavate the beingness in ourselves and others, we are going to get our hands dirty; our heads may even become jumbled and jarred. The important thing is to commit to never letting your heart get scared as the under-the-surface toxins manifest. Also, you don't want to be unwise and begin your dig without the necessary, essential protective gear and equipment to safeguard you from the elements. Just like you wouldn't go out in the rain without an umbrella and perhaps rain boots and a hat, don't embark on a people or organizational excavation without praying for and activating your spiritual awareness and discernment, making sure your emotional and organizational intelligence are high, gathering a skilled and diversified team, and being certain that you can live with what you discover. In making these final investments, know you will may have to commit to helping bring health, healing, and wholeness to those impacted by this literal and figurative removal of dirt.

LITTLE DRUMMER BOY

Growing up, my brother, BJ, dabbled around with playing the drums at our local church. Depending on the season, he was more committed to learning how to play and honoring his commitment to the church youth group than at other times when sports, hanging out, and just finding his way were more of a priority. While BJ was a fun-loving, jovial, and light-hearted kid, intrinsically he battled with the rejection of his biological father who remarried and wasn't an active part of his adolescent life. Church and the drums were the balm and bond that stood in the gap and brought some healing. Probably around age 13 or 14, someone he looked up to and trusted breached that bond by openly criticizing him in one of his Jesus or "kickin'-it-with-my-boyz" seasons. Over time, that slight morphed into hurt. Ultimately, the enemy of our souls flipped the script, that hurt turned into offense, and my brother stepped away from organized religion altogether.

BJ became "that guy" who loved God but couldn't really stand His hypocritical people. For years, conversations about organized religion and church were relatively one note. While we had deep discussions about life, love, forgiveness, and reconciliation, conversations about him giving God a second look through the local church were not the business (something he was open to talking about at that time). Fast-forward to the summer of 2015, July to be exact. Holy Spirit had put it on my heart to have direct conversations—about salvation—with two people whom I loved dearly. One of those people was my brother. Now 34 years of age, he was the father of an 8-year-old son and 1-year-old daughter. I remember we were about to hang up after having solidified plans for my nephew Benjamin, Jr., aka Kellz, to come to Atlanta to spend time with me and his Uncle Mo. I begin to awkwardly circle back around to our usual twice-a-year conversation about his reconsidering connection in the fullness of God (Father, Son, Holy Spirit).

A lot of the details of our navigation around the subject are fuzzy because when I finally got the courage to pivot to salvation, my brother excitedly cut me off. He said words that even to this day bring me great joy and comfort: "Sis, you probably won't believe it, but I've been watching Pastor Joel Osteen and that Boi Good!" We both chuckled at my brother using slang. Saying, "that Boi Good," was a huge compliment. He went on to say, "I got you, Sis. I actually gave my life to Christ a couple of weeks ago, and I feel so much better and have so much hope." As the ugly cry commenced, all I could say was, "Wow, Bro. I am so happy for you. It's the best decision you could have ever made for you and your children." It's still hard to fully make sense of that conversation and all that happened afterwards, since on November 19, 2015—a little more than a week before his favorite holiday, Thanksgiving— my brother passed away suddenly and unexpectedly. With no prior major medical issues, he transitioned from life to life in the Kingdom.

There isn't a day that goes by that I don't miss my little drummer boy. BJ had a way with people that has left a void in all of our hearts and minds—especially his son's and daughter's. While I may never get comfort on this side, I'm thankful I went on the excavation dig that July to unearth the gold. I can be at peace because in time I will unequivocally see him again.

PARTICIPATE, OBSERVE, AND LEARN

If you are going to be an effective cultural anthropologist, immerse yourself in the organizational environment as a participant, observer, and learner. In doing this, you gain first-hand experience without up-line filtering and editing of the promises and problems of the environment in which you lead. You are also able to garner trust and respect from those who usually see you as inaccessible or out of reach. In effect, you do as former President Roosevelt admonished. You get in the game by stepping into the arena to participate in the making and shaping of being-as-leading environments. In his famous "Citizenship in a Republic" speech given at the Sorbonne in 1913, he reminds us that the "man" we should admire is the one who is willing to fight the big battles even if they end in defeat.

It is not the critic who counts—not the man who points out how the strong man stumbles, or where the doer of deeds could have done them better. The credit belongs to the man who is actually in the arena; whose face is marred by dust and sweat and blood; who strives valiantly; who errs; who comes short again and again because there is no effort without error and shortcoming; who actually endeavors to do the deeds;

who knows great enthusiasms and great devotions; who spends himself in a worthy cause; who—at the best—knows in the end the triumph of high achievement, and who—at the worst—if he fails, at least fails while daring greatly, so that his place shall never be with those cold and timid souls who neither know victory nor defeat.

In her groundbreaking and culture-shaping work on vulnerability and shame, sociologist turned life coach Brené Brown offers a remix of President Roosevelt's "Man in the Arena" speech. She writes,

> When we spend our lives waiting until we're perfect or bulletproof before we walk into the arena, we ultimately sacrifice relationships and opportunities that may not be recoverable, we squander our precious time, and we turn our backs on our gifts, those unique contributions that only we can make …. Perfect and bulletproof are seductive, but they don't exist in the human experience (Brown, 2015, p.13).

We are living in some of the most volatile and uncertain times in world history. From the hyper-sensitivity and weaponization of our thoughts and words to the economic recession that stimulus checks and PPE loans can only keep at bay for so long, the current health, financial, political, emotional, racial, and personal crises and disruptions we face seem insurmountable. Yet, the ability to stay afloat has less to do with what is currently in our bank accounts and more to do with how we gain access to, read, lead and navigate these turbulent times and climate. So often, the ability to be the leaders God called us to be can be swayed, undercut, or compromised by nonstop and constantly changing headline news. These seemingly never-ending reports of tumultuous political, financial, environmental, and societal changes, challenges, and upheavals can make even the greatest being as leading leader question his or her motives, mission, and mastery of the people and organizations he or she leads. As a leader, when you incorporate participation, observation, and learning into the day-to-day operations, structure, and leadership of your company, it's no longer about your personality and preferences, it's about the principles and perspectives you want all of your employees to follow, model, and replicate for others.

LISTEN WELL

One of the most effective ways to unearth the gold in your environment is to listen well. In listening, you are exercising Stephen's Covey's #5 Habit: "Seeking to understand and not be understood." Unfortunately, most of us listen with the intent of replying for the purpose of being understood. As Covey stated,

If you're like most people, you probably seek first to be understood; you want to get your point across. And in doing so, you may ignore the other person completely, pretend that you're listening, selectively hear only certain parts of the conversation or attentively focus on only the words being said, but miss the meaning entirely. So why does this happen? Because most people listen with the intent to reply, not to understand. You listen to yourself as you prepare in your mind what you are going to say, the questions you are going to ask, etc. You filter everything you hear through your life experiences, your frame of reference. You check what you hear against your autobiography and see how it measures up. And consequently, you decide prematurely what the other person means before he/she finishes communicating (Covey, 2004, p. 281).

One of the easiest ways to do this is by borrowing the cultural-anthropology methodology of participant observation where you intentionally immerse yourself into the day-to-day lives of the people and culture you are observing and sharing in. Participant observation happens when a researcher or investigator gains access and social acceptance into a group of people. The cultural anthropologist, in turn, intentionally creates closeness and community as a way of collecting data to get a fuller, more complete understanding of the internal structure and sequence of that society. I know leaders who do this well and others who haven't a clue how to do this at all. There are a few traits I've personally observed in those who do this well.

First, they use observation to connect divergent thoughts and perspectives about the organization. To be clear, it isn't just the use of visual observation. These leaders have effectively incorporated the power of active listening in their engagements and assessments. In a nutshell, they listen well. In being as leading, to listen well, they try to hear with an ear bent towards understanding in an effort to gain clarity on the heart issues at play. These leaders also listen well to ensure that the care, safety, and wisdom of all parties involved remains at the forefront.

I love what organizational psychologist Adam Grant, author of *Give and Take*, *Originals*, and *Option B*, recently tweeted: "We listen too much to people who think fast and shallow, and too little to people who think slow and deep. Being quick on their feet may make them smart, but it doesn't mean they are wise." I think he'd agree with the Good Book and its instructions in James 1:19 to "Understand this, my beloved brothers and sisters. Let everyone be quick to hear [be a careful, thoughtful listener], slow to speak [a speaker of carefully chosen words and], slow to anger [patient, reflective, forgiving]" (AMP).

LISTENING WELL IN ACTION

As leaders, when we commit to and put into practice the power of listening well without interruption, criticism, or cynicism, we create leadership cultures where problems, challenges, and even failures can be brought to our attention early and often. The compounded effect of this type of culture is a place where honesty, transparency, and integrity are cultivated in the hearts as well as infrastructure of everything that is created. If we want to be known as those who lead well, I believe we must first be known as those who listen well. If we are going to listen well, we have to commit to the following actions:

1. Be present mentally, emotionally, and spiritually.
2. Be especially aware of your facial expressions and eye contact.
3. Be open to new thoughts, ideas, and expressions.
4. Be discipled to listen with both head and heart.

5. Be disciplined to not interrupt or interject.
6. Be willing to give a recap of what you have heard.
7. Be disciplined to not give an immediate reaction or make any promises.
8. Be willing to admit when you were wrong.
9. Be willing to clarify needs and expectations.
10. Be willing to excavate the truth.

When we do these things well, we not only create culture, we multiply and exponentially replicate culture.

DO YOU SEE WHAT I SEE?

Another thing you have to do if you are going to become a cultural anthropologist within your environment is be willing to observe your environment both up close and behind the scenes. One of my favorite guilty pleasures is to watch scripted reality TV shows that fight for the underdog. To me, the show Undercover Boss did just that as CEOs, who wanted to get an up-close-and-personal look at their companies, left their corner-office suites and took it to the streets and front lines of their companies. In stepping outside of their comfort zones and going into the daily zones of their "essential" workers, managers, and middle-level leaders, these undercover bosses were able to see what their workers see: the good, the bad, the ugly, and even the hypocrisies in mission, vision, morale and execution within their organizations.

In adopting a posture of "Do you see what I see," you don't practice what my former Pastor Byron Broussard calls the "Ministry of Amazement." In practicing the ministry of amazement, you either are truly surprised by the dysfunction, drama, or top-down powered relationships usually driven by control, pride, and ego, or you feign such "amazement" to absolve yourself of any responsibility in turning a blind eye to the environmental culture and leadership dysfunctions. Either way, usually these dysfunctions are a direct result of *laisse-faire* leadership and management or a failure to inspect what you expect of those who are in executive and leadership roles within your organization, company, or church. These types of hands-off leadership models tend to foster atmospheres where being as leading is never established or can't take flight. The end result is that most people walk around impotent and unable to be all that God created them to be. Instead of operating in the *Imago Dei*, they usually end up mimicking the Imago Me of the loudest, most critical, most opinionated, most controlling manager, leader, or supervisor in the place.

INSPECT WHAT YOU EXPECT

Now that we've explored the significance of participation and observation in leadership environments, I want us to conclude with a discussion of the role of learning and how it impacts being as leading. One of the areas of participant observation in which cultural anthropologists acknowledge caution is needed, is in the realm of behavior. In particular, they have to be aware of and able to make the distinction between ideal, actual, and believed behavior. The breakdown of these three human and social behaviors are as follows:

Ideal Behavior—What we think we are doing and want others to believe we are doing
Example: I am the hardest working person.

Actual Behavior—What we are really doing
Example: I work hard on some projects or assignments.

Believed Behavior—What we honestly believe we are doing
Example: I am working harder than anyone else.

All these of these learned behaviors are significant but can be deceptive if not closely observed, monitored, and inspected to ensure that the cultural anthropologist is gathering the data expected. Why? More often than not leaders have the ability to be misled because people may not be sure of what the leader wants. People then present themselves, the organization, or even data and outcomes from a framework that doesn't fully reflect the reality of the organizational culture. To guard against both conscious and unconscious skewing and positive spin, a leader has to figure out how to read the pulse of the culture. By inspecting what you expect, a leader or his or her assigned proxy is able to measure, assess, evaluate, and retool more readily because he or she is already immersed in the environment and can make strategic pivots and principle-centered leadership shifts.

A leader who manages change through the inspect-what-you-expect model priorities the people, values, and morale of the organization over its titles, positions, and practices. More often than not, these types of leaders aren't afraid to make changes to the organizational culture beneficial to its end game. You can do many practical things to inspect what you expect within your organization:

1. Establish clear expectations.
2. Reinforce these expectations early and often.
3. Convert these expectations into organizational values.
4. Incorporate these expectations into organizational and leadership handbooks, manuals, and codes of conduct.
5. Engage and create accountability systems for employees and leaders at all levels of the organization.
6. Recognize and celebrate those who excel at replicating these organizational values and expectations.
7. Develop programmatic tracks, trainings, and talks to reinforce these organizational expectations.
8. Do not allow changing cultural tides, opinions, or beliefs to shift or diminish your expectations.
9. Share these organizational expectations with other community or corporate stakeholders.
10. Repeat steps 1-9.

While there will be potential start-up costs to incorporating these steps into your environment if they don't already exist, the return on dividends of doing them is exponential. More importantly, this type of environment has the potential to create an atmosphere of exponential self-actualization—what psychologist Carl Rogers calls the "fully functioning" person. In his work on human psychology, On Becoming A Person (1961), Rogers argued that in order for people to develop and grow, they need to be in environments that are first of all genuine, then accepting, and finally empathetic. Combined, these environmental attributes create self-actualization where one's ideal self is in alignment with one's actual self to create a fully functioning person. These people are "in touch with their deepest and innermost feelings and desires."

FOLLOW ME

ON DECEMBER 25, 2019, musical mastermind and Yeezy sneaker brand genius Kanye West released his highly anticipated Sunday Service Choir album. In many respects, this Christmas gift to the world, a remix of his Pablo album—an electronic and techno fusion "gospel" inspired project—was groundbreaking. The album served dual notice of Kanye's musical re-awakening as well as his public declaration of now being a Christ follower. In interviews, he shared his radical salvation experience which happened while making Jesus is King—the rap album he released earlier in the same year.

As he shared at his "Sunday Service" at New Birth Missionary Baptist Church outside of Atlanta, "You sent your son to die for us and all you ask is for radical obedience to you. You're not asking us to do the least. You know how people are like, at least I …how are we gonna do the least when he did the most?" Continuing in his thoughts, he lamented, "I've seen him work miracles in my life…You know the devil presents so many flashy, shiny objects. I've seen everything that the devil could've showed you via TV, videos, car dealerships, jewelry, houses, and I'll tell you... Nothin' beats God... and a sound mind" (*ajc.com*).

When we, like Kanye West, invite others to engage in "Follow Me" being as leading culture, we are providing an open door to where we currently find ourselves in authenticity, transparency, and clarity. We are also acknowledging the evolutionary processes of discovery and change that have brought us to our current place of compassion, consciousness, and—perhaps—even new birth.

FOLLOW ME?

Anyone remotely familiar with Kanye West and his notorious rants of self-aggrandizement and self-professed greatness is rightfully skeptical of this new believer. Is this new-to-the-club Jesus freak legit? Or is this "Closed on Sunday" lyricist selling the gospel to gullible millennials a 2020 Presidential election run slick PR trick? With tracks like "On God," "Everything We Need," and "Follow Me," the married father of four, advocates God over culture, family and fidelity over fame, and simplicity over superficiality yet his public meltdowns and constant twitter rants has the entire world watching and praying to see what happens next. Still, in an interview affirming his faith, he said, "Let's not be concerned with the opinions of men at all. Only the opinion of God. I know we say this is the culture or that is the culture. To be radically in service to Christ is the only culture that I want to know about." Hopefully, this cultural tastemaker and disruptor who proclaimed Jesus healed him can stand the test of time. More importantly, I pray that critics and Christians alike will model a semblance of his boldness, his unapologetic sway, his refusal to dim his light even if it's a mere shadow of an encounter with Christ.

Today the spotlight is on Kanye West and whether or not he puts his faith in Jesus, his Anchor to the ground, his Hope and Firm Foundation, the only One who will never let any of us down. However, the reality is that for many of us Christ followers, our focus shouldn't be on Kanye or any of his catchy promises. Our focus should be on how we navigate and manage change just like Jesus did when He gave the invitation for the disciples to follow Him.

While there at least 58 scriptures that give the invitation to follow Jesus, we know that not everyone who received the invitation of Jesus became a Christ follower. The simple truth is that if people rejected Jesus, they will also reject the leadership of you and me. Such a sobering reality must be what compels us forward in organizational and leadership progression and keeps us out of the never-ending cycle of maintaining the status quo which will slowly produce organizational paralysis and regression. Whether we are going to be leaders who issue the Kanye version or the Matthew 4:18-20 version of "Follow Me," we have to be willing to give up some things in order to level up in the ability to create cultures others want to replicate and "relay."

On "Follow Me," Kanye's Sunday Service Choir melodically harmonizes,

Follow me, follow me
Follow me, follow me
Follow me, follow me

Follow me, yeah, follow me
We're hoping to see the day
That our people, can all relay
We must keep strivin' to achieve the peace
If we just keep believin', we shall all be free

In the Kanye version, when one does as instructed to "Follow me," there is hope "that our people, can all relay" which means to receive, spread, transfer, and pass on information to others. While there is no direct reference to Matthew 4:18-22, it is difficult to imagine that the track is devoid Christ-consciousness as part of the hook reads, "If we just keep believin', we shall all be free." Similarly, yet distinctly different, Matthew 4:18-20 (AMP), also calls for an exchange of sorts. It reads,

As Jesus was walking by the Sea of Galilee, He noticed two brothers, Simon who was called Peter, and Andrew his broth-er, casting a net into the sea; for they were fishermen. And He said to them, "Follow Me [as My disciples, accepting Me as your Master and Teacher and walking the same path of life that I walk], and I will make you fishers of men." Immediately they left their nets and followed Him [becoming His disciples, believing and trusting in Him and following His example].

In this great exchange, Jesus unapologetically offers freedom from the status quo to these two fishermen—brothers Peter and Andrew—in exchange for their willingness to leave their nets and security nests in pursuit of Him.

The call to "Follow Me" is more about what is to come and less about what has been. In today's time, imagine Jesus walking into a local coffee shop and encountering two day traders who just so happen to be brothers. Before they can take another sip of their white chocolate mocha lattes, Jesus says, "Follow Me, and I will make you developers of men." In issuing this same call today, leaders have to be clear about their objectives and outcomes so that others are aware of what is at stake if they are to follow the leader.

Legendary, old-school hip-hop icon Eric B said it this way in the track with the same name:

> I can take a phrase that's rarely heard
> Flip it now it's a daily word
> It's a danger zone, he should arrange his own
> Face it, to space it, grace it, change the tone
> —"Follow The Leader," Eric B and Rakim

In order to create a replicative follow-me and follow-the-leader culture, it is important to have a clear understanding of where you want your company or organization to go and what your key areas of needed growth are. In effect, you have to create a culture where everyone is able to "Walk it like I talk it." However, in order to do that, you have to have a clear understanding of the characteristics, contaminates, and considerations that are actively present in the culture.

GOT CULTURE?

If someone were to ask you, "What are the predominant characteristics of your culture?" what would you say? Do you lead and live in a peaceful, harmonious, Christ-conscious culture, or are you a part of an antagonistic, hostile, and competitive culture? Is your culture fast-paced, high-intensity, and demanding, or is it a laid-back, passive, and chill environment? If in fact, you are a culture of one, your organization should reflect your heart, your value, your vision. If it doesn't, you will need to take some time to investigate who or what is drowning out your heartbeat from being synchronized and replicated in the leadership space. I asked chef and doula, Chelsia Ogletree, owner of Her Majesty, Inc., what culture speaks to her. She shared,

> Culture to me is a recipe from Grandma's kitchen that came from her grandma's kitchen that came from her grandma's kitchen and is now in my kitchen. Culture is the passing down of curated art, dance, lessons, and ways of being from generation to generation. Culture is rich in layers of shared experiences, and influences one's being.

> I shape my New Orleans Creole culture as a leader in my home by celebrating highs and lows. Accepting obstacles as a challenge to endure with grace and being lovingly resilient displays my culture in my home. My culture shapes my leadership as a youth minister in that we believe in taking care of our "babies," teaching them and embracing their personalities, letting them know that they are loved and accepted. I encourage my fellow leaders to be unapologetic in ministry, yet loyal to the cause of the gospel.

> In my work as a chef and restaurateur, the Creole culture is woven into every aspect of operations. First, being loyal and

having integrity not only to the execution of a Creole recipe but to the customer and to the business. Dancing in the kitchen and the sharing of stories as we prepare meals can be found every time the stove is lit. —@chefchelsiadoula (IG)

VICTORY MIDTOWN

Almost two years ago, my husband, Mo, and I became pastors of the Midtown campus of Victory Church. The campus, in the heart of the arts, entertainment, and business center of Atlanta, had its own flavor and flow. It is well-known and embraced that while every campus of Victory Church (Midtown, Norcross, Hamilton Mill, and Online) follows the organizational culture model of simplicity, sincerity, and sacrifice as well as the 4 Pillars of Building Families, Transforming Communities, Impacting Nations, and Reconciling Cultures, each campus has its own unique personality and feel. For the first six months of our pastoral journey, Mo and I became cultural anthropologists and immersed ourselves into the Victory Midtown environment. We did this in order to observe, learn, listen and build rapport with the preexisting team, congregants, and surrounding community.

Once we were clear on the preexisting cultural characteristics, we prayerfully sought the Lord and guidance from our leaders about the ways we needed and wanted to reshape the culture. For us, we wanted the culture to be known for three things: leadership, serving and community. We started with our team by incorporating weekly leadership lessons into our staff meetings. For the first year, Mo did the majority of these teachings as he is a certified John Maxwell leadership coach. Today, the entire team rotates these weekly leadership teachings. We also incorporated "On the Spot" prayer. Culturally, what this means is that when someone asks, "Can you pray for me?" we will pray with a person in the moment, on the spot. On the spot prayer is just one of many things we do to foster community.

During COVID-19, Mo wanted to extend our culture of care and build intentional community even though we couldn't physically gather. He shared that he wanted our team to call the entire Midtown-campus congregation. Keep in mind that our team is evenly split between extroverts and introverts. While some on the team were excited, others temporarily died on the inside. We began calling, and the connection, testimonies, and gratitude we received were so positively overwhelming that we shared them with our senior leadership team. In sharing with the global leadership team, the decision was made to extend this initiative to all of our campuses. As a global organization, Victory Church called over 22,000 members. More importantly, the leadership gold still being circulated as a result of this intentional act of care has been priceless. In a global pandemic, our church has been able to be a blessing to front line and essential workers, nonprofits, schools, families, and people in need all around the world while blessing our local members through a host of initiatives including virtual small groups, online membership, and corporate prayer and worship every Wednesday evening.

WHAT ABOUT YOU?

Without having to look anything up or call your assistant, in order of importance, can you list your organizational culture characteristics or values? Use the space below to list them and detail why they are important to you.

MY TOP 5 ORGANIZATIONAL CULTURE CHARACTERISTICS

1. _____

Why? _____

2. _____

Why? _____

3. _____

Why? _____

4. _____

Why? _____

5. _____

Why? _____

I asked you to write down your organizational cultural characteristics and values in the last section because research has shown that writing things down lends itself to more intentionality, commitment, clarity, and focus. It also helps us to crystallize what we say we believe and ensure that systems are in place from both a leadership and management perspective to reinforce expectations and outcomes. For example, if you say you value people, your environment will speak to this truth through the systems and practices in place. If you say you value profits, the systems in place will also speak to this cultural characteristic.

CULTURE SPEAKS

Believe it or not, every organizational environment speaks both verbally and nonverbally through the culture it creates as well as the space it makes to prioritize what it says it values. How often have we heard of upset, frustrated people who are held to standards organizational leaders ignore, disregard, or violate? I often reflect on the common practice of ethical atheism and the "Do what I say not as I do" culture that is predominant in seemingly every area of life. As cultural anthropologists, we must be painstakingly careful to recognize, correct, and close any ideological or ethical gaps in the idealized self/organizational cultural in comparison to the actual self/organizational culture we perpetuate.

PEOPLE OR PROFIT?

One of the most debated topics of this entire pandemic has been about people and if we truly value them. Let's just deal with the underlying elephant-sized question in the room which has plagued us since the beginning of time. Who and what do you value? More specifically, how do you articulate what you value, and can this value be quantified over time? If the proof is in the pudding, one can trace who and what we value to the time, resources, and emphases we place on certain areas. Arguably, the same formula can be applied to see where there is an absence or lack of value especially if there are no measurables, metrics, or quantifiable objectives that speak to the alleged value.

For many, the seemingly profit-centered rush to "reopen" and return-to-normalcy hysteria fostered by many politicians, business leaders, and entrepreneurs did not speak to a leadership culture that added value to others. In particular, authorities have exhibited an absence of clarity regarding whether or not front line essential workers including medical doctors and hospital personnel, government leaders and officials, law enforcement and safety personnel, as well as a host of service-industry workers (cashiers, waiters, bus drivers, and ride share operators) should wear PPE—personal protective equipment. If so, people remain unclear if companies will provide such. These issues and if employees, fearful of contracting the virus, may take time off without penalty have been widely documented. As the death toll has mounted and public pressure has increased, some companies have been forced to prioritize people over profit.

It seems that COVID-19 has caused many people to take a closer look at their values as it has forced nearly every sector in the nation and the world to shut down and pivot both people and resources to address the new social-distancing norms. While I believe history books will record the highs and lows of how the international community processed the pain and new normal of the pandemic, I think there will be an even greater narrative birthed of how people intentionally leaned in to create follow-me cultures focused on paying it forward, going the extra mile, and lending a helping hand. Remember, opportunity abounds to set and shape culture as well as give people an up-close-and-personal look at what we value especially during times of uncertainty, crisis, and change.

Companies like Nike and Apple took the lead by issuing statements that valued and prioritized people over profit margins. Nike may one day prove to be an interesting case study of a corporate follow-me culture as the company has done an exceptional job being as leading and shaping culture in two globally significant areas: COVID-19 and honoring, supporting, and valuing the lives of brown and black people. Here are the company's press statements. Notice the language used to connote value. While some can question the timing of these statements, the intentionality communicates valuing others.

NIKE PRESS RELEASE ON COVID-19

For the continued safety and well-being of our teammates and customers, our Nike owned and operated stores will remain temporarily closed in multiple countries around the world. Stores in select locations are open based on guidance from health and government authorities. Customers can find information on stores here.

NIKE PRESS RELEASE ON BLACK LIVES MATTER

Today NIKE, Inc. is announcing a $40 million commitment over the next four years to support the Black community in the U.S. on behalf of the NIKE, Jordan and Converse brands collectively. This commitment will be focused on investing in and supporting organizations that put social justice, education and addressing racial inequality in America at the center of their work. Systemic racism and the events that have unfolded across America over the past few weeks serve as an urgent reminder of the continued change needed in our society. We know Black Lives Matter. We must educate ourselves more deeply on the issues faced by Black communities and understand the enormous suffering and senseless tragedy racial bigotry creates," said John Donahoe, President and CEO of NIKE, Inc. "The NIKE, Inc. family can always do more but will never stop striving to role model how a diverse company acts. We will continue our focus on being more representative of our consumers while doing our part in the communities we serve. We believe in a level playing field for all and leveraging the power of sport and our brands to move the world forward. This additional $40 million builds upon the NIKE, Inc. family's long history of providing support to the communities in which they operate. We are deeply committed to driving focus and impact through our teams, brands and community partners.

•••

Did the company or organization you lead or work for issue similar statements? If so, did you feel valued and cared for? Did they boost your morale and increase your productivity, or did the statements or absence of such cause more confusion and uncertainty about the leadership culture and environment in which you work? Lastly, what did the statements fail to say that causes you or co-workers to question how your company or organization sees and values you?

THE MARSHAWN LYNCH EFFECT

As a leader, have you ever just had a bad day where you weren't feeling it, and everything—big or small—rubbed you the wrong way? Have you ever been cranky, tired, or just irritable and taken those feelings out on others? Have you ever just had a day that you were "over" before you even got out of the bed? If you responded, "Yes," to any of those questions, CONGRATULATIONS! and welcome to Leadership 101. All jokes aside, the weight and burden of leadership can be so heavy at times that it can morph and suck the life out of one's ability to lead from a place of authenticity, transparency, or joy. In these moments, it can be very easy to point out the mistakes or mishaps of others while being blind to one's own inability to create a being-as-leading, follow-me culture. We can become so caught up in a "You should be glad that I'm here," or an "I'm doing you a favor," mentality both of which have a negative ripple effects everywhere we go. Leaders and people who aren't just having a bad day but live in a constant state of "I'm doing you a favor by being here" and do the bare minimum operate in what I like to call the Marshawn Lynch effect also known as the "I'm just here so I don't get fined" philosophy and mindset.

For those of you not familiar with this eight-word viral phrase, let me give you some history. During the 2015 Super Bowl media day, Lynch a running back for the Seattle Seahawks, fielded questions with some variation of the response, "I'm just here so I don't get fined." According to *ESPN.com,* for 4 minutes and 51 seconds, Lynch dodged 29 questions. "About 200 reporters crowded around Lynch's podium for at least 15 minutes before he arrived. But Lynch wouldn't answer any questions. He set a timer on his phone, caught a bag of Skittles tossed from the crowd and stopped to pick up a reporter's recorder off the floor before he walked out." Lynch's dislike and disengagement with the media had been well-known and documented. In 2014, at a similar media event, Lynch was reported as saying, "I'm just 'bout that action, Boss."

I'm aware that the Marshawn Lynch effect is an extreme example of defiance that no one hopes is present within his or her leadership culture and environment. However, if in any way you foster or allow others in leadership to foster a culture of negativism, sarcasm, passive-aggressive behavior, antagonism, hostility, entitlement, visceral reactions, and even bullying, you could very well knowingly or unknowingly be responsible for creating an environment where people just show up so they won't get fined.

OBLIQUE VS. OBVIOUS THINKING

Another way you can create a healthy being-as-leading, follow-me culture is by introducing oblique thinking into your environment. What is oblique thinking? Dr. Sam Chand, author of New Thinking, New Future, describes it as a way of thinking that is cutting-edge in its innovation as it combines both strategic and genius thinking. It is a model of thinking that functions best in being able to think in and through obscurity, ambiguity, and unknowns. He writes,

> Some might ask, which is better, strategic thinking or genius thinking? The answer is both. Like two wings of an airplane, leaders need both to thrive. As an organization grows larger and more complex, leaders need to engage in oblique thinking. A few leaders are comfortable with ambiguity. They don't insist on guaranteed outcomes for their biggest decisions. In fact, they relish the challenge of charting a course through unsettled waters (Chand, 2020, pp. 24-25).

The oblique thinker knows that the answer may not be discovered linearly and more than likely will come through discovery and experimentation. So many people in our environments are limited in both their thinking and their creativity because we aren't comfortable with fostering environments that are creative and allow people to think outside of the box. Our environments don't allow for the answer to come to us as we journey together without guarantees or promises.

Conversely, many of us operate and rely heavily on what I call follow-the-directions, color-within-the-lines, obvious thinking. It's linear and logical and largely remains in a safe zone that has very little to do with overall organizational structure. It's stagnant and predictable. It routs our ways of thinking, our systems, and the people within our environments. The end result is that we don't allow for the limits or lids to be blown off and refitted for the current needs, asks, and wants of the organization. Take a look at these examples of obvious thinking, and ask yourself if you have ever been limited, capped, or forced to settle for comfort and convenience relying on one of these schools of thought:

We've always done it this way.

It's just easier this way.

If it ain't broke, don't fix it.

Ain't nobody got time for that.

They like it like that.

Why bother? They never notice.

The added value of incorporating oblique thinking into one's organizational fiber is that it becomes a part of the DNA of the culture. So many of us have been trained to engage in and toe the line of obvious thinking that we don't even know that WE DON'T KNOW what we're missing by way of innovation, productivity, and even organizational positivity. So many of us have been in environments or been the keepers of the guard of man-made preferences, traditions, and routines. On a lighter note, think about how many of us don't do certain things, don't eat certain foods, and won't have certain experiences and interactions because we didn't "grow up" with certain social norms or expectations in our households. As a child, I remember always wondering why we never shared the same utensils or drinking cups in my house.

To this day, I have never shared the same cup, bowl, or utensil with my siblings, mom, or dad. It was so ingrained in me, in such an obvious yet unexplainable way, that when I married Mo, and he'd ask for a bite of my burger or a sip of my sweet tea, I'd look at him like he'd lost his mind. I'd give my best side-eye (translation: Nah bruh! You need to get your own.). He'd look at me and say

"REALLY, ARE YOU SERIOUS?" My point is this: I was so stuck on my obvious way of thinking that was part of how I grew up that I had never even entertained that others might operate differently. Scientifically, I am certain my mom's adamancy of not eating after others has some validity. However, her obvious rules of engagement related to this excluded any possibilities for ambiguity or exceptions to the rules (including my future husband, lol).

MY FOLLOW-ME CULTURE

We've spent some time examining what a follow-me environment could look like. Now, take a moment to create your own. In the space below, do three things. First, revisit your Top 5 Culture Characteristics and Values. Next, write a paragraph that captures these sentiments and why you champion such within your sphere of influence. Lastly, take what you've written and send it to at least five people within your leadership sphere with whom you want to connect and intentionally add value to in this season.

Dear _____,

_____

_____

_____

_____

_____

chapter 7

LOVE AND COVER OTHERS

The end of all things is near. Therefore be alert and of sober mind so that you may pray. Above all, love each other deeply, because love covers over a multitude of sins. Offer hospitality to one another without grumbling. Each of you should use whatever gift you have received to serve others, as faithful stewards of God's grace in its various forms. If anyone speaks, they should do so as one who speaks the very words of God. If anyone serves, they should do so with the strength God provides, so that in all things God may be praised through Jesus Christ. To him be the glory and the power for ever and ever. Amen. —1 Peter 4:7-12 (NIV)

SERVE OTHERS AS FAITHFUL STEWARDS

ON TUESDAY, FEBRUARY 25, I flew home to Providence, Rhode Island, to check on and spend some time with my mom. Both my sister and I had become concerned about some identified and some unidentified health challenges she had faced with what felt like rapid-fire intensity for a little over a year. The sudden death of my brother only deepened our concerns, so I shared daily check-ins and up-close care which, until this time, my sister Funmi had predominantly handled. While our mom, Jackie, is a characteristically strong woman, the past year had been filled with a mixed array of emotions. We've watched her navigate a new normal where she has needed more love and covering from us. Everyone who has journeyed down this road knows the awkward dance of trying to parent your parents.

Being the master over thinker that I am, I wrote down all the things I considered to be her next steps and what I wanted to get done during the days I was home. During my first 24 hours at home, in between online lectures on Gentrification, Political Parties, and Vulnerability in Leadership, I realized that something was terribly off. Honestly, it was more like I was off. While my head was in the game, and I was checking my list and getting things done, my heart was still far away. It was tucked away in its protective shell of being, from the inside out, unwilling to let my true emotions—fear, anxiety, worry, and uncertainty—show as we considered my mom's future. No one could question my physical presence. I went into firstborn-responsibility mode taking her to doctor appointments, sibling visits, and the grocery store. Even as a short order cook, I prepared fresh meals for her breakfast, lunch, and dinner. However, being present physically doesn't mean anything if you are absent emotionally, psychologically, empathetically, and spiritually. To make matters worse, I knew I wasn't fully present which only added to the head-versus-heart dilemma I was internally battling all while attempting to do for my mom.

In a moment when I should have been pastoral and walking out the instructions in 1 Peter 4:7-12, I was being professorial and operating in the letter of the law—not the spirit of the law. I found myself back on auto-pilot because I grew up living in two worlds: my head and my heart. In my head space, I was always smart, dependable, responsible, reliable, practical, and self-reliant. My mom could count on me to get things done and never "stay in my feelings" for too long. I learned early that I needed to observe more than ask questions to gain perspective so as not to create any problems. I did this very well. I excelled in school, in sports, and even in leadership at the Allen A.M.E. church where I grew in my faith in God after accepting that invitation from my friend Jameela.

In my heart, however, I was a completely different person. In my heart, I dreamt of Oh, The Places [I'd] Go! as I lost my introverted self in reading whatever I could put my hands on: magazines, newspapers, articles, or books. I dreamt of all of my imaginary friends around whom I could just be my organic, natural, and shy self. I dreamt of my two left feet somehow finding rhythm and dancing like no one was watching. I dreamt of being in environments where I could be the point guard—one who can make the shot but gets just as much joy out of making an assist so my friends can win. I dreamt of my own family and the intentional environment I wanted to foster with abounding safe places and spaces. In effect, I dreamt of an older me—free from societal, familial, or self-imposed restrictions that didn't allow me to breathe. I dreamt of being all God created me to be where I could—in both head and heart—experience and truly live out the mandate to "above all things" have intense, unfailing love because love forgives and disregards the offenses of others.

Standing in the middle of my mom's kitchen, making a Southwestern chicken salad for her lunch, I had a come-to-Jesus moment. In what felt like an hour, but actually was only a few minutes, I was reminded of the girl who would pick up the brush and start preaching when everyone left the house, the girl who never made a big deal about her birthday so as to not get in the way, and the girl who took four buses a day to get to the most prestigious school in the city in order to create a path of greater opportunity beyond graduation day. In that moment, I decided that I wasn't going to live in the old tomb of non-emotionalism and routine; I was going to get in the game and wear my heart and emotions on my sleeve. I was going to live, love, and laugh in my mom's home like no one was watching. I was going to be all that God called me to be while serving her and trusting Him to order all of our steps. On that day, I decided to let my head and heart align as I recommitted to love and cover my mom.

LOVE AND COVER OTHERS

One of the things I was reminded of is that until we face what has hindered our ability to be, we can't effectively love and lead others. While it's convenient and safe to function on autopilot at times to mask prior hurts and disappointments, numbing and self-medicating are only temporary fixes. They fail to excavate or get at the core of what's within us that needs a shift in consciousness, compassion, and conviction. When we give ourselves permission to be—to flow in the essence, spirit, life, and reality of whom God has formed, fashioned, and wired us to be—we accept the challenge and responsibility of leading ourselves well knowing that the opportunity frees us to also lead others. The transformative nature of being someone who is willing to do the work required to lead from a place of being is that its fruit remains in your life and becomes a replicable mainstay in the lives of others.

Are there areas in your life where your ability to lead from the core and essence of your being is limited, hindered, blocked, or knowingly compartmentalized? Are there some areas that you are unconsciously numbing or dumbing down to go along to get along? Do you have a public self that is on autopilot and a private self who dances like no one is watching? No matter where you find yourself, now is the time to take action to close the gap between the two in your journey of self-discovery. In order to this, you have to be willing to make some considerations:

1. Be willing to examine your own self-protective thoughts and actions.
2. Be willing to honestly examine your expectations, motives, and needs.
3. Be willing to recognize when you are going into a safe zone or shut-down mode.
4. Be willing to acknowledge the triggers that activate your self-protection mechanism.

5. Be willing to concede that there is a side of you that you aren't expressing and a reason why you are afraid to fully be.

6. Be willing to create a safe space with God where He can enter into these numbing areas.

7. Be willing to invite others you trust to hold you accountable when you find yourself hiding out within yourself.

8. Be willing to give up this unhealthy defense mechanism so you can grow in healthy life-giving mannerisms.

9. Be willing to observe someone else being all that God has created that person to be and invite him or her to mentor you up close or from afar.

10. Be willing to begin again when you find yourself reverting back to old ways of being because of fear, anxiety, misperceptions, anger, or new triggers.

If we are going to serve others as faithful stewards, we must each first attend to and be the faithful steward of our own soul. In this regard, we must be willing to acknowledge, accept, and hold ourselves accountable to the truth of the Word of God and our values, core beliefs, accountability partners, and God-wiring.

One of the greatest joys and sources of fulfillment in my life is being in the lives of the students I teach. I've been blessed to be a full-time professor at a large research university—The University of Georgia—and a small, private liberal arts institution—Oglethorpe University—where I currently serve as Chair of the Division of Politics, History, and International Studies. Over the years, I've taught some of the best and brightest young people, many of whom are lawyers, doctors, doulas, city planners, elected officials, researchers, teachers, and accountants. Every year, I am blown away at their prowess. They are confident, they are courageous, and they are clear on what they want. Yet, every year, I pause and lament at what I observe: While these students make up a generation of some of the most creative and intellectually advanced minds ever, some of these beautiful minds are being robbed by both internal and societal pressures. Anxieties and injustices chip away at their ability to be.

OFFER HOSPITALITY WITHOUT GRUMBLING

I remember one of my students from my early years at UGA. A brilliant mind, fascinated by African American culture and studies, she talked with an accent that was not her native tongue. From Vermont, it was as if she felt she had to put on a demeanor and speak in the dialect of someone else to justify her authentic passion and pursuit of social justice. My semesters always seemed longer when I read her name on my enrollment roster. I'd heave a deep sigh and mutter, "Here we go again," when entering class. It's ironic that in all of her efforts to be someone else, she also challenged me since she didn't believe that "someone as smart, beautiful, and intelligent as [I] should be a Christian."

I remember the day she shared her thoughts on my faith during an in-class discussion. That all eyes were on me is an understatement as her 49 peers watched to see my response. I remember thinking to myself, Thanks, God. Literally, here we go again. I honestly don't remember what I said in response that day. I do know I was at my wits' end because I felt like I was striking out as it related to offering hospitality without grumbling. It really doesn't matter because what I will always cherish and remember is the day everything about our dynamic changed. At the time, my office was on the third floor of an old building without an elevator. As you can imagine, most students asked to meet anywhere but there. On that particular late afternoon, I wasn't even expecting anyone since it was my last day at UGA. I had accepted a professorship at Oglethorpe University.

My door was ajar, so when I first heard the gentle knock, I assumed it was one of my colleagues. I looked up, and to my surprise it was that student. Again, I thought to myself, Come on, God! You can't be serious. It's my last day here! I tried to put a smile on my face as I invited her to have a seat. After some small talk about the class and my future plans in Atlanta, she said she needed to tell me why she was there. She went on to share how for two years she had taken every class that I taught because she'd made it her personal agenda to get me to denounce my Christian beliefs. She said she purposefully tested me and even deliberately did things like talking in a particular dialect or using slang to provoke me to lose it in front of others. She said she did whatever she could to ruffle my feathers to see if I was just faking it or frontin' (being inauthentic) because she didn't believe my faith was real. She said, "You actually are who you say you are, and if the God you serve can allow you to be at peace, then I want Him in my life too." On that day, I was able to love and cover her.

Today, she is a civil rights attorney who loves and covers the families of black boys and men who have lost their lives due to senseless acts of racism and violence and the refusal of people to—above all else—love others. For me, I am in awe of God. My willingness to lead from my place of being—even when I intrinsically didn't want to and at times felt like I had failed—was all part of His divine plan for me to love and cover her until she accepted Christ and His plan for her life.

COVERING?

Many of us can argue we are good when it comes to loving others. It's Christianity and even Humanity 101. We understand the power of agape love. We know that we are to hate the sin but love the sinner. We even acknowledge the karma, negative energy, and ways in which not loving others can kill our vibe. In many respects, when it comes to loving others, I think many of us would say, "We good. We got that," with the fullness of the meaning the usage of slang is intended to convey. My question then is this: How are you doing with covering others? Yes, you can check off the box of being a leader who "loves" everyone. However, are you a leader who understands the transformative power of covering everyone?

LOVE COVERS A MULTITUDE

What does it mean to cover? To cover means to protect, shield, cloak, and mantle. It means to place something over or upon to conceal and to protect. It also means to serve as a substitute or to fill in the gap. I think we can all agree that today we are witnessing one of the greatest parental and family gaps in the history of our society. With so many children, teens, and young adults coming from dysfunctional homes—even in the body of Christ—multitudes are in need of and looking for someone—regardless of that person's title or position—to genuinely cover them. They need people willing to roll up their sleeves and go the extra mile with them emotionally, psychologically, and spiritually. They need your love and cover even when they "Heisman" you and act unlovable.

Today's youth need people in their lives that honor, value, and cover them for who they are—not just for what they can offer. They need people in their lives who aren't impressed with their performance-driven natures but who encourage them to take off the culturally-induced façade of "Fake it 'til you make it." I remember telling one of my mentees, "It doesn't matter what you say to try to push me away. I'm not going to let you stay locked up in old ways of thinking and performance-based connection and leading." In a 2018 American Psychological Association journal, the Psychological Bulletin, Dr. Thomas Curran connects the increase in performance-based behavior in millennials and young adults to "social media, perfectionism, and meritocracy." He writes that "meritocracy places a strong need for young people to strive, perform, and achieve in modern life." This, in turn, is causing a "rise in perfectionism among millennials." The end result is that the young people of this generation bear a much heavier burden of anxiety, depression, and suicidal thought patterns than their predecessors. This weight, I believe, can be lightened by those in connection with them who are willing to love and cover the multitude of issues they face. Simply put, we've got to do more than just "preach." It's time to pair our preaching with methodologies and practices that are able to speak to, love, and cover the unreachable and the hateful—those like my former student looking to knock out confessions of faith.

CONNECT AND DON'T CONDEMN

All of this sounds simple and poetic, right? Honestly, leading from this place of being is one of the hardest tensions I have to manage because there are times when I have to be more vulnerable than I want to be in leading. I have to face the potential of being rejected as a leader. And, I have had to heal from being hurt by those I've been entrusted to lead. Whenever I've struggled to lead from my being in these areas and even when I have been hurt, I've come to realize that it's usually because I was "doing" more than I was "being" in my leading. In a practical sense, whenever I've found myself either struggling to lead from a place of authenticity and vulnerability or I have been disappointed or hurt by someone in leadership or someone I was leading, it usually has been the result of my unwillingness to trust my gut (discern, read, and heed the warning signs) or my eagerness to get ahead of where the person was or where God was leading. The irony of it all, is that the apostle Paul gave us a being-as-leading cheat sheet.

I planted, Apollos watered, but God [all the while] was causing the growth. So neither is the one who plants nor the one who waters anything, but [only] God who causes the growth. He who plants and he who waters are one [in importance and esteem, working toward the same purpose]; but each will receive his own reward according to his own labor. For we are God's fellow workers [His servants working together]; you are God's cultivated field [His garden, His vineyard], God's building. —1 Corinthians 3:6-9 (AMP)

Another being-as-leading principle we can apply from the apostle Paul is to connect with others instead of condemning them. I believe part of why we are faced with so many divides today—racial, political, economical, social, and cultural—is because far too many of us show up with our preconceived freeze-frame narratives of what we think and believe about people and culture. Instead of leaning into people and learning about their history, we find ourselves superimposing value, worth, and even dignity based upon how we secretly see, believe, and rank them. And, we get our ideas from what the media or our favorite politician, leader, or friend has said about others with similar experiences.

I asked Brooke Hempill, Senior Vice President of Barna Group, how she sets or shapes culture within the environments she leads. She shared,

When I study culture in my work, I mostly think of the culture of the world—as Paul studied the culture of cities before taking the gospel to the people in Acts. So, my perspective is more one of studying culture and helping interpret it for church leaders. However, it is impossible not to build a culture whenever you are leading—and even sometimes when you are following! Internally in my organizational role, culture looks like making Barna Research an awesome place to work! I want my team to have opportunities to stretch and grow, try new things, and take on responsibilities. I want them to know they are valued and have something that is "uniquely them" to bring to our team.

I also know that work can be hard—especially in ministry, where spiritual trials are for real! So, we PRAY—A LOT!—and we work to build a culture of trust and encouragement to weather storms together. In order to develop and attain these cultural norms, we have to be explicit about them and state and share that this is what we're working towards. We have to practice them by developing habits and traditions that build up our "muscles" in these areas (like taking retreat time to reconnect at least twice a year) and getting creative with new ways of reinforcing these norms ("quaran-team virtual happy hours").

And, we have to keep reminding each other. It's easy to get distracted or out of habit. Usually after our annual "culture survey," we find we've veered off-track and have to revisit some of our practices—like going on a diet again. And amidst it all... there's A LOT of grace, because our human selves will mess up, and we'll inevitably disappoint each other. But we stay grounded in our shared faith and our shared purpose. —@barna_brooke (IG)

As indicated, connection, community, and commonality of shared experiences—in this instance faith and purpose—are key.

As unintentional as it may be, every time we fail to connect first from a place of genuineness and seeing others through the *Imago Dei,* there are intentional consequences that may be irreparable. It's why I want us to remember the words Paul shared. In 1 Corinthians 9:22 (AMP), he reminded us of the posture needed to effectively lead and reach those in need. He wrote, "To the weak I became [as the] weak, to win the weak. I have become all things to all men, so that I may by all means [in any and every way] save some [by leading them to faith in Jesus Christ]."

When we connect and do not condemn, we are able to high-light the intersectionality, interconnectedness, and agency associated with our good, good Father and His reckless love toward not only us but people all around us who need to be covered and loved. In doing so, I've been able to connect and not condemn students at some of the most liberal and con-servative academic institutions in the nation.

A CASE STUDY—THE SECULAR AND THE SPIRITUAL

Last year, I spoke at San Francisco State University, and while my topic—Being Is Leading: The Transformative Leadership of Beyonce and Cardi B.—may make many of you reading this book question if I've been water baptized, God used that topic to open the door and glorify himself at one of the nation's most liberal universities. As is common and a very gracious part of the way God allows me to come to grips with some of His wiring of my being, I did my usual tango when I first sensed His presence. Once I realized He wasn't going away, we began to do the two-step that I've grown to understand simply means that when He moves, I move—just like that.

In the midst of my presentation on how these two artists have actualized their respective personal agencies, He gave me spot-on words of knowledge and wisdom for five of the campus influencers in the room. Honestly, it blew my mind probably more than those of the people who received the prophetic words because until that point there had been a negative chain reaction of events including arriving at 1am PST. Everything that happened leading up to those "God winks" was designed to make me condemn and not connect. I had triggers, alarm clocks, sirens, and even tornado warnings going off in my heart and mind giving me permission to go inward, to protect myself, to allow my doing to overtake my being. I wanted to let the man-made offenses take precedence when God wanted me to just be—allowing the offenses to not attach to me—so He could lead me and set people I may never see again on a new course of discovery and freedom.

And my personal, spiritual leadership OG (Original Gangsta), the apostle Paul reminded me,

> The end of all things is near. Therefore be alert and of sober mind so that you may pray. Above all, love each other deeply, because love covers over a multitude of sins. Offer hospitality to one another without grumbling. Each of you should use whatever gift you have received to serve others,

as faithful stewards of God's grace in its various forms. If anyone speaks, they should do so as one who speaks the very words of God. If anyone serves, they should do so with the strength God provides, so that in all things God may be praised through Jesus Christ. To him be the glory and the power for ever and ever. Amen. —1 Peter 4:7-12 (NIV)

If you haven't figured it out yet. Choosing to lead from a place of being takes vulnerability and courage. At times, it will cause you to get cut and bleed.

These are the facts: It's the truth; yet it always yields life change. You don't do it because everyone is doing it. You yield to it because truly it is today's road less traveled. It's the balm we have to heal our land. It flows from the place of being and resting in Him as we look to create and shape culture that isn't influenced by the mounting tensions, pressures, conflict, and unrest that are ubiquitous in our society.

chapter 8

THE 3 M'S: MINDSETS, MICROAGGRESSIONS, AND MISUNDERSTANDINGS

W E'VE ALL HEARD the saying, "Change is inevitable." I've lived long enough to wholeheartedly agree with that statement and to wish that a counter-balancing truism would have been shared more frequently as well. I get it. Change is unavoidable, widely accepted, and welcomed. We have songs, books, TED Talks, movies, podcasts, churches, organizations, and social media platforms dedicated to this six-letter word. I wish we'd begin to highlight and give just as much attention to another word that is equally as—if not more—important in helping us to create as well as navigate change in our environments. That word is "conflict." Conflict is also an inescapable part of our leadership, workplace, and family life. It's a part of culture. Given its dominant role especially in our current COVID-19, to-wear-or-not-to-wear masks, to-open-or-not-to-open business and schools, 2020 politically plagued society, I wish we'd be more open to acknowledging that "conflict is inevitable." Conflict is certain because at its base and safest level, it's merely a difference in perspective of how two people view the same situation. At its worse, however, conflict has been the source of war, violence, and death.

From an organizational and leadership standpoint, I wish we'd talk more about avenues where people can discuss as well as resolve conflict, so it doesn't persist, fester, and spread. I wish we'd talk about the fact that conflict without resolution is harmful. I wish we'd talk about what unresolved and internalized conflict does to the human soul and body. I wish we'd talk about how it torments the mind and creates disease similarly to what Dr. Curran's study on millennials and perfectionism revealed. What I have found to be true from both observation and scientific research is that conflict—a powerful, pernicious, and pesky eight-letter word—can be detrimental and destructive to even the most positive strategies we implement in our spheres of influence.

In its Workplace Culture Report 2020, Emtrain analytics noted the following:

Many managers are unaware of the implications of their power on social dynamics at work, and the impact it has on how others behave. Without a strong feedback culture, power can be abused, where certain people consistently get away with bad behavior—including discrimination and harassment.... Strong, positive norms correlate with a healthier, more inclusive environment that is better at regulating in-appropriate behavior and more resistant to culture-failures. When there aren't strong norms in an organization, significantly fewer employees rate their organization as healthy... and only 32% of employees strongly agree that they can be their authentic self in the workplace.

The dataset consisted of 2.5 million responses collected from 40,000 employees across 125 plus companies. The Workplace Culture Diagnostic also linked workplace conflict to six key indicators. The first set of indicators applies to individuals: unconscious bias, social intelligence, and preexisting mindsets. The second set is made up of organizational indicators: in-groups/out-groups, power dynamics, and norms and practices. The research also pointed to a hot-button issue in the workplace—politics. The reality is that workplace culture breeds known and unknown conflict, and over a five-year span costs companies $223 billion in lost revenue, destruction of property, sick days, and harassment law suits.

On a positive note, the Emtrain study strongly suggests that employees can be taught to learn how to engage in healthy conflict resolution. The study noted that an absence of healthy organizational culture, coupled with toxic managers and middle-level employees, is the reason why employees leave and attracting and maintaining top talent can be difficult. If we are going to lead from our being, we have to deal with the detrimental affect and effects of culture. More importantly, we have to create safe environments where conflict is welcome and resolved. In order to do this, we have to look at some of the root causes of conflict—mindsets, microaggressions, and misunderstandings—and reimagine how we can productively use these oftentimes toxic commonalities within our organizations, family spheres, friendship groups, and society.

MINDSETS

3M is a well-known global brand touted for its innovation and collaboration which has produced some of the most technologically savvy supplies, materials, and creations on earth. With over 100,000 patents, it proudly identifies itself as a company committed to improving the lives of others through science, technology, and marketing. "Today, more than 60,000 3M products are used in homes, businesses, schools, hospitals and other industries. One-third of our sales come from products invented within the past five years, thanks to innovations from the thousands of researchers and scientists we employ around the world" (*3m.com*). The history and humble beginnings of this multinational Fortune 500 corporation exhibit many rich life and leadership aspects. The one that I want to focus on above all others is mindset.

What is one's mindset? A mindset is a set of beliefs, attitude, or mental state of being. It's a way of seeing the world based on both past history and experiences as well as current realities. Dr. Carol Dweck, author of The Growth Mindset describes two types of mindsets—fixed and growth. Those with a fixed mindset believe a person is born with certain innate predispositions. Those with a growth mindset believe that hard work, applied thinking, and input from others can propel people forward. In effect, I'd liken those with a growth mindset to people who possess PMA—positive mental attitude. These are the people who always see the cloud's silver lining, the situation's bright side, and the cup as half full.

Often a person's mindset can be shaped by negative, traumatic, and painful experiences from childhood that he or she brings into the work environment or organizational leadership culture. It can also simply be a by-product of the last experience that person had with someone trying to switch lanes on the highway. As the Emtrain survey indicated, people enter into workplace environments shaped by their pre-existing mindsets, unconscious bias, and social intelligence. As developers, shapers, and molders of organizational culture, we have to be aware of those factors which can produce mobilization bias or negative groupthink. We also have to be willing to examine and ask critical questions about the current culture in place. Reflect on the following questions:

1. What are the powered positions in our organizations?
2. Who occupies these powered positions?
3. Why do they occupy these powered positions?
4. Are those occupying these powered positions the most qualified (intellectually, socially, emotionally, and spiritually) to do so?
5. Are we raising up others to serve alongside those in powered positions?
6. Are we analyzing issues of diversity, inclusion, and parity in our organizations?

7. Are we examining both unconscious and conscious bias in our hiring, promotion, and mentorship practices?

8. Are we bringing in experts in the field to holistically address needed areas of growth, improvement, and cultural shift?

9. Are we listening to the informal conversations of staff, contractors, and current and former employees?

10. Are we creating safe spaces of transparency and transformative dialogue?

Additionally, we need to utilize transformative leadership and people mechanisms to bolster positivity, workplace leadership development, and mindset shifts that reflect the current leadership and organizational DNA. Making our priorities and perspectives clear and more prominent than any of the negative culture-conflict undercurrents will result in refinement of vision as well as an alignment of the organization to your being as leading practices and philosophy. If there aren't any current crises or conflicts within your organization, you can also strategically realign organizational priorities and values to speak to your values, beliefs, and mindset.

I am actually witnessing and participating in this type of positive organizational mindset shift at my university. Our 17th President, Dr. Nicholas Ladany has a rich history of and commitment to diversity, equity, and inclusion. On his first day as our leader, he penned an open letter to the Oglethorpe University community. In it, he shared his values and beliefs which will lead to a shift in positive organizational and cultural leadership.

MICROAGGRESSIONS

If you have ever heard someone say or been told things like "You are a credit to your race," "Gender plays no part in whom we hire," or "I didn't expect someone with that last name to look like you," you have experienced microaggression. At their core, microaggressions are a form of subtle and not-so-subtle racial stereotyping or racialized responses meant to demean, judge, exercise power over, and/or—ironically—even compliment someone who is a member of a historically subjugated or oppressed people group. Jenée Desmond-Harris wrote in the 2015 article, "What Exactly Is a Microaggression,"

> Microaggressions are more than just insults, insensitive comments, or generalized jerky behavior. They're something very specific: the kinds of remarks, questions, or actions that are painful because they have to do with a person's membership in a group that's discriminated against or subject to stereotypes. And a key part of what makes them so disconcerting is that they happen casually, frequently, and often without any harm intended, in everyday life.

In the same article, Desmond-Harris gives historical context on the origination of the term. Mircoaggressions was coined in the 1970s by Harvard University professor Dr. Chester M. Pierce to capture the insults and slights witnessed against African Americans. He wrote,

> These [racial] assaults to black dignity and black hope are incessant and cumulative. Any single one may be gross. In

fact, the major vehicle for racism in this country is offenses done to blacks by whites in this sort of gratuitous never-ending way. These offenses are microaggressions. Almost all black/white racial interactions are characterized by white put-downs, done in automatic, preconscious, or unconscious fashion. These mini disasters accumulate. It is the sum total of multiple microaggressions by whites to blacks that has pervasive effect [on] the stability and peace of this world (Sue, 2010, p. 26).

Growing up in Rhode Island, I learned how to manage microaggressions at a young age. I remember the first time someone commented, "You're so articulate." The person thought it was a compliment. I just smiled and kept repeating the word to my 9-year-old self so that I wouldn't forget to look it up. I also learned early on to not take offense at people's ignorance whether it was intended or unintended. The problem, however, is that not everyone has my demeanor or experiences. Not everyone has the patience or the Christ-centeredness to turn the other check toward microaggressions. Further, not everyone is able to choose their Christ culture over their race, ethnicity, or national culture. As a result, even in the body of Christ, we aren't loving and covering each other as we are admonished in 1 Peter 4:7-12. We too, have engaged in negative mindset shift, microaggressions, and even misunderstandings that have resulted in both public and private quarrels, unforgiveness, and unwillingness to be leaders who will lay down our "stones" of judgment.

In our organizational environments, we must be leaders who are willing to go first by educating ourselves about microaggressions and other types of divisive speech and thought that are both historically and presently harmful to our cultures. We also must go beyond educating ourselves to equipping those around us—especially those who serve in powered positions—to combat such. Lastly, we must inform everyone within our spheres of influence that such contentious and destructive behaviors aren't welcomed or tolerated. Microaggressions, like most issues, ultimately can be traced to the power dynamic in relationships and perceptions of others. Political scientist, Thomas R. Dye, likens it to politics and power. He believes, "Political science is about power and its distribution—in particular, who gets power and by what means, when, and how?" (Dye & Guy, 2008, p.18) I think we can ask the same questions within our society, organizations, leadership groups, and even churches. Ask yourself,

1. Am I open to innovation and change?
2. Am I focused on authentically empowering others?
3. Am I willing to "go to bat" for others by utilizing my power and influence?
4. Am I willing to have "hot mic" conversations?
5. Am I willing to advocate on behalf of others when no one else will?
6. Am I willing to fight for empowerment, diversity, and inclusion publicly and privately?
7. Am I willing to challenge the organizational status quo?
8. Am I willing to examine where change is needed?

9. Am I committed to implementing said change?
10. Am I willing to share my power, influence, and resources for the sake of change?

MISUNDERSTANDINGS

Depending on what your day has looked like so far, you've already had a misunderstanding. It may have happened before you even got out of bed because you and your spouse didn't see eye to eye on something. It might be that email titled "MORE CLARITY NEEDED." It might be that cryptic text, "Got a sec? Need to talk." Maybe it's none of these things. Maybe its confusion at the intersection as you tried to get over and someone lost their everlasting mind on their horn and supernaturally learned sign language to ensure you had a good day as they waved you on. Whatever the scenario, if you are still living and breathing, you've had a misunderstanding with someone about something at some time in your life. A misunderstanding is a mix-up, an absence of clarity, a difference of opinion, or an error in perception, alignment, or expectations. And misunderstandings are caused by many actions:

1. An absence of clarity in communication
2. Quick, fast, or fractured communication
3. Siloed or segmented communication
4. Assumptive or agenda-oriented communication
5. Passive-aggressive communication, speech, or behavior
6. Partial or fractured listening
7. Disinterested or distracted engagement

8. Writing, reading, or responding to texts, emails, or calls quickly
9. The absence of margin (at least 24 hours) to respond
10. MULTI-TASKING

I share these to remind us all to slow down, take a break, wait, and even pray before we respond so as to not create additional rifts, tensions, or unintended consequences or actions that further aggravate our environments.

As an academic, I religiously follow a few procedures to try to bring clarity and avoid misunderstandings in my courses. First, I do my best to communicate, communicate, and communicate. In particular, I communicate early. Before the start of the semester, I send a welcome email to my classes and lay out the academic journey. Second, I use inclusive language such as "we" and "us" to steer away from top-down communication. Third, I provide the books and materials needed ahead of time. In doing so, students are able to get a head start on the content. Fourth, on the first day of class, I use the entire class period to cast vision, chart our course for the 16-week semester, answer questions, and reassure the students that we are in this together. Lastly, at the midpoint of the semester, I take half a lecture period to recast vision. During this time, I also encourage students to persevere (as now its midterm-examination time) as well as reset expectations, goals, and outcomes.

How do you manage conflicts in your organizational environment? In what ways do you reshape and reset culture that may be challenged by negative mindsets, microaggressions, and misunderstandings? In the space below, detail what you want to do to begin to foster healthy organizational culture that reflects your values, vision, essence, and being?

Chapter 9

EQ, GQ, AND YOU!

WE FOCUS A lot on A person's IQ (intelligence quotient). However, if we are going to create healthy, transformative, and pay-it-forward leadership cultures, we must provide a blueprint for how to overcome leadership-culture corruptors and replace them with leadership-culture creators and multipliers. EQ (emotional quotient), GQ (God quotient), and the YOU quotient are that blueprint.

EMOTIONAL QUOTIENT

Currently, EQ is all the rage. Most widely known as emotional intelligence, the term was coined in 1990 by researchers Peter Salovey and John D. Mayer. Described as "a form of social intelligence that involves the ability to monitor one's own and others' feelings and emotions, to discriminate among them, and to use this information to guide one's thinking and actions." Dr. Daniel Goleman (1995) added four additional qualifiers to this ground-breaking work. He described emotionally intelligent people as possessing the following attributes:

1. Self-awareness
2. Self-management
3. Social-awareness
4. Social Skills

Now, more than ever, we need leaders who operate in EQ. These leaders, who are congruent in head and heart, aren't afraid to lead from a place of "True North" authenticity. Today, we need leaders who utilize their social awareness, social skills, self-awareness, and self-management to help diffuse the anger and pain that lead to vitriol and other effects of absent leadership evident throughout our nation and world. We literally need leaders who, regardless of political ideology, theology, race, culture, and creed, will—in spirit and truth—commit to go high when others go low. We need modern-day Joan of Arcs: men and women who are willing to burn at the stake of uncompromised values and beliefs, speaking up and speaking out for the voiceless, the powerless, and the disinherited of the earth.

If you have ever felt like a figurative Joan of Arc, take heart and comfort now in the words of the apostle Paul from The Message. In Philippians 4:1 and 8, he wrote,

> My dear, dear friends! I love you so much. I do want the very best for you. You make me feel such joy, fill me with such pride. Don't waver. Stay on track, steady in God. ...Summing it all up, friends, I'd say you'll do best by filling your minds and meditating on things true, noble, reputable, authentic, compelling, gracious—the best, not the worst; the beautiful, not the ugly; things to praise, not things to curse. Put into

practice what you learned from me, what you heard and saw and realized. Do that, and God, who makes everything work together, will work you into his most excellent harmonies.

To all of my modern-day Joan-of-Arc, being-as-leading leaders, please take heart in knowing someone has to be the pioneer and leader of change.

I caution you to exercise wisdom, practice patience, and count the cost as many who should speak up, advocate alongside you, or champion the cause given their powered positioning won't do so publicly. They will, however, want to commiserate privately. There are times you may be convicted by calling to do what is right. Other times, you may be motivated by more of a sense of purpose or the desire to foster healthy belonging. Whatever the motivation, check it. If its ego-driven or egocentric, lose it because it will reproduce its own destructive and devisive fruit. If it's rooted in the truth of Philippians 4:1 and 8, then keep talking about it, keep advocating for it, and keep doing what you can do to manifest it because at some point the truth will take root.

GOD QUOTIENT

Referred to by a few names such as faith quotient, spiritual quotient, and wisdom quotient, I define our God quotient as our ability to be in sync, in step, and in tune to the presence, purpose, call, wisdom, and direction of God in our lives. To me, our GQ is our innate, internal, and divinely aligned navigational system that leads, directs, and guides us. It is a combination of applied knowledge and wisdom working in tandem alongside intuition and discernment. A person's GQ is his or her ability to have the mind of Christ on matters and apply His wisdom to the difficult and divisive discourse of the day. For centuries we have heard about IQ. While one's intelligence quotient remains the most traditional standard of aptitude, the measurement of one's cognitive ability in comparison to one's age doesn't always equate to the development and emergence of leaders who are healthy, whole, and fit to lead well.

As shared in chapter 2, intelligence is one of several characteristics associated with the trait theory of leadership. However, IQ alone isn't enough to foster positive people and organizational change. Again, The Message, this time in Proverbs 19:21, states it best: "We humans keep brainstorming options and plans, but GOD's purpose prevails." We need more GQ to quell some of the entitlement, emotionalism, dividing lines, and ignorance that has been fueled by humanism, cultural relativism, and sectarianism. Today's reality is that everyone is "woke" and can sense, feel, and ascertain if you truly "walk it like you talk it."

YOU!

Now more than ever, leaders have the opportunity to "Be the Change" they seek in the world. Where established politicians, pastors, celebrities, and influencers are pledging allegiance to different sectors, parties, and divides, there is an entirely new intergenerational squad of emerging leaders which is setting aside ego and pride. These leaders are putting their power, resources, and influence behind the causes and campaigns that strive to heal hearts and unite people amid the loudest distractors—some of whom profit from the chaos, confusion, and economic, political, racial, social, and cultural divides. Our power lies in our willingness and ability to not sit by and hope for, but act, create and cultivate leadership, organizational, and societal change. Dr. Martin L. King, Jr., said it like this: "If I cannot do great things, I can do small things in a great way," and "Change does not roll in on the wheels of inevitability but comes through continuous struggle." More pointedly, in his 1963 "Letter from a Birmingham Jail," he wrote what remains one of the greatest rebukes of the modern church on issues of racial reconciliation and healing:

> We will have to repent in this generation not merely for the vitriolic words and actions of the bad people, but for the appalling silence of the good people. We must see that human progress never rolls in on the wheels of inevitability. It comes through the tireless efforts of and persistent work of men willing to be co-workers with God, and without this hard work time itself becomes an ally of the forces of social stagnation. We must use time creatively and forever realize that the time is always ripe to do right (King, 1964, p. 21).

NEXT STEPS: STAKEHOLDERS, PARTNERS, AND GAME CHANGERS

I doubt that a year ago, the majority of us were thinking that a global pandemic would change the very nature of how we conduct business, obtain education, enjoy live music, fellowship with our families, or even worship God. Yet, here we are prayerfully watching and waiting as entertainers, professional athletes, law enforcement officials, and even mayors of major international cities have been diagnosed with COVID-19. Many of us have been forced to slow down and wait and be still and know. Others have had to examine and reevaluate the rate at which we've allowed ourselves to run ourselves into the ground in the name of our calendars, appointments, and the seemingly never-ending demands of the day. As historical and modern-day racialized brutality have made it to the front page, I believe we've also had a front-row seat to emerging as well as established stakeholders, partners, and game changers who will continue to lead from their authentic and innate places of being even after the headlines fade and the cameras stop rolling. These traditional as well as nontraditional leaders, cultivators, and shapers of culture are those who are leading from a place of being.

MILLENNIALS

According to the Pew Research Center, four significant indicators capture the character of the millennial. First, there is an age component. "A millennial is anyone between the ages of 22-37 in 2018." Second, there is the political component. Most millennials came of age during "politically polarized" times wherein the "Rock The Vote," "Rap The Vote," and "Vote or Die" campaigns significantly bolstered the youth vote. Third, millennials grew up during the 2008 recession which has delayed their development in the realm of financial independence. According to a 2019 Pew Research Center report,

Beyond politics, most Millennials came of age and entered the workforce facing the height of an economic recession. As is well documented, many of Millennials' life choices, future earnings and entrance to adulthood have been shaped by this recession in a way that may not be the case for their younger counterparts. The long-term effects of this "slow start" for Millennials will be a factor in American society for decades (Dimock, 2019).

Lastly, millennials are shaped (some contend a bit too much) by technology since they witnessed the launch of the iPhone, apps, and other technological advances.

As a result of these four phenomena—especially the utilization of technology—this generation appears to rely on Google more than God, text more than they talk, and have more followers on social media than some churches in America have parishioners in their pews. Still, God is speaking to and through the triumphs and tribulations of millennials. Chance the Rapper is just one of many through whom I believe God is shining His light to raise awareness of the highly flawed yet saved-by-grace humanity that is the DNA of all who bear the *Imago Dei*. In this regard, I believe that "for such a time as now," it is also important to understand the seeming ease as well as angst of millennials. On his track "Blessings," he unapologetically declares that while he stumbled and fell as a result of age, politics, economics, and technology, in this moment he can say,

I made it through, made it through, made it through
And everything I gave to you, I gave to you, I gave to you

You got it, you got it, you got it, it's coming (Coming,
　　coming, coming)
So are you ready?
Are you ready?
Are you ready for your blessings?
Are you ready for your miracle?
Are you ready for your blessings?
Are you ready for your miracle?

Say what you will about millennials. Even with their commitment phobia, shortcomings, and failures, they have been the
ones on the frontlines, taking it to the streets, reminding us all to
"Say Their Names"—Breonna, Floyd, Ahmaud, Elijah, and even
Emmett (Till).

MUSIC MAKERS

Music is one of the most powerful influencers of global culture. Why? Music creates connection, incarnates consensus,
and crafts culture. No matter where you find yourself—
Madagascar or Miami—there is a sound that emanates from
particular places and spaces that speaks to what is current
and more importantly what is coming through the interconnectedness and intersectionality of sound. Kanye West,
Maverick City Music, Lauren Daigle, Kierra Sheard, Lecrae,
Tasha Cobbs Leonard, and Elevation Worship, in my experience, are all part of this intergenerational sound that has
swept across the nation and is producing unprecedented
numbers of "on earth as it is in heaven" Kingdom of God

worship experiences that flow in the Galatians 3:28 mandate. Elevation Worship's 2016 release "Here As In Heaven" captures it best,

> A miracle can happen now
> For the Spirit of the Lord is here
> The evidence is all around
> That the Spirit of the Lord is here
> A miracle can happen now
> For the Spirit of the Lord is here
> The evidence is all around
> That the Spirit of the Lord is here

RACIAL RECONCILIATION

I believe anyone with ears to hear and eyes to see can recognize the move of God happening through the landscape of racial reconciliation in the Kingdom of God. While there remains work to be done to heal the church's political polarization that has shaped the last three election cycles, there is one undeniable trend on the uptick within the body of Christ—racial reconciliation as leadership realigns. In this regard, one of the most significant keys in the area of racial reconciliation has been the "Here as in Heaven" oneness through worship that is neither black nor white, Jew nor Gentle but focused solely on the transformational power of Jesus Christ.

Interestingly, I believe these unprecedented levels of universal sound brought about by Christ-centered Rainbow Coalition worship experiences are also creating 21st century "first-evers" in the body of Christ. Consider these noteworthy two:

1. Younger African American pastors are legitimately and legally receiving sizable and significant churches and schools from established long-standing white pastors.

2. Racial Reconciliation Movements such as "OneRace" (*oneracemovement.com*) gathered over 70,000 people on Stone Mountain in 2018 "to renounce the historic divisions of racism, and petition God for racial reconciliation and revival in our nation." More recently, in the 2020 March on Atlanta on Juneteeth, over 10,000 people lamented, repented, and committed to next steps of righteousness, justice, and reconciliation.

INTERGENERATIONAL MINISTRY

Another area I believe God is speaking in "for such a time as this" is the realm of intergenerational leadership. For far too long, the church has been sorely divided on issues of race, gender, and age. While most churches have waded patiently through the waters of racism and sexism, ageist tendencies as well as the rise of seeker-friendly philosophies have cost our nation the experience of multiple generations worshiping and leading together. While across the board, church attendance is down (online and streaming church services are up), it is interesting that intergenerational ministries that focus on worship, serving, and leading being a family affair have not experienced the same type of drastic membership and attendance shifts.

The question for some is, "What exactly is intergenerational ministry?" According to Holly Allen and Christine Ross, "Intergenerational ministry occurs when a congregation intentionally brings the generations together in mutual serving, sharing or learning within the core activities of the church in order to live out being the body of Christ to each other and the greater community."

I personally can attest to the power and transformational leadership of this model via my local church: Victory Church founded and lead for 30 years by Pastors Dennis and Colleen Rouse. Pre-Covid, On any given Sunday, our children's ministry serves 1,350 kids through the volunteer efforts of 1,000 members—two of whom were my husband, Mo, and I before we became pastors of the Midtown campus. The Rouses have committed their hearts, minds, and resources to building a church focused in part on reconciling cultures. In a 2018 sermon series entitled "One Race," Pastor Dennis shared,

> Jesus was called the rock of offense when He spoke. When He spoke, although He spoke the truth, not everybody agreed with the truth because they were so enculturated with their human culture. They didn't understand the truth beyond that. Here is what is happening. What's happening in America has been happening down through the centuries. As culture has established itself around the world, we have begun to worship our human culture over God's Kingdom

Culture. We've formed entire religions, political persuasions, and church culture around our human culture, and we've made it an idol. Wise is the person who chooses His Kingdom Culture over earthly culture.

Today, because of their commitment to put Kingdom Culture over human culture, Victory Church is home to people from 142 nations who worship, fellowship, and do life together.

IN SUMMARY

Every day we, ourselves, have the opportunity to model being as leading. Every day we have a chance to shake off what others and society say about who we should be and embrace the *Imago Dei* and the truths about whom God predestined, fashioned, and set us in place to be. It doesn't get any clearer than Jeremiah 1:5 (MSG), "Before I shaped you in the womb, I knew all about you. Before you saw the light of day, I had holy plans for you: A prophet to the nations—that's what I had in mind for you."

Being as leading is our opportunity to create a new dawn and horizon of change designed to shift culture by lifting each other through heart work, healing, and holistic organizational leadership and culture change. It's an opportunity to examine the past, inspect what we expect, say something when we see and sense things are not as God intended, lift as we climb, cultivate others to sit in powered seats and positions, and champion the causes of others. Being as leading isn't just the right thing to do. In the words of gospel group Mary Mary, "It's the God in me," and you—in both of us—leading us to do it.

When we lead from our being—a place of knowledge and belonging that brings clarity, wisdom, perspective, and peace—we are able to face our fears and acknowledge that we are powerful beyond belief because we have been purposed on earth to lead from a place of truth as described by Marianne Williamson in her timeless classic *A Return to Love: Reflections on the Principles of A Course in Miracles*. She writes,

> Our deepest fear is not that we are inadequate. Our deepest fear is that we are powerful beyond measure. It is our light, not our darkness that most frightens us. We ask ourselves, "Who am I to be brilliant, gorgeous, talented, fabulous?" Actually, who are you not to be? You are a child of God. Your playing small does not serve the world. There is nothing enlightened about shrinking so that other people won't feel insecure around you. We are all meant to shine, as children do. We were born to make manifest the glory of God that is within us. It's not just in some of us; it's in everyone. And as we let our own light shine, we unconsciously give other people permission to do the same. As we are liberated from our own fear, our presence automatically liberates other (Williamson, 1992, p. 97).

When we accept the call, the command, and even the challenge of leading from our being—from the *Imago Dei* and all its splendor—we too, create atmospheres, environments, homes, workplaces, and cultures that allow people to develop, blossom, and soar. In being in our leading, we embrace the freedom and liberation that comes from God ordained knowingness, authenticity, and originality. In so doing, the spirit of the living God alive in us creates opportunities and even uses pandemics and other types of global disruptions where our being—our unique perspective, imprint, stamp, and DNA—is set apart, ordained, and called to create, shape, and reimagine culture, leadership, future forward and transformational organizational change.

WORKS CITED

BOOKS

Allen, Holly C, and Christine L. Ross. (2012). Intergenerational Christian Formation: Bringing the Whole Church Together in Ministry, Community and Worship. Downers Grove, IL: IVP Academic.

Brown, B. (2015). Rising strong (First edition). New York: Spiegel & Grau, an imprint of Random House.

Chand, S. (2019). New Thinking, New Future. Pennsylvania: Whitaker House.

Covey, Stephen R. (2004). The 7 Habits Of Highly Effective People: Restoring The Character Ethic. New York : Free Press.

Desmond-Harris, Jenee. (2015). What Exactly Is A Microaggession? D.C.: Vox.

George, Bill, and Peter Sims. (2007). True North: Discover Your Authentic Leadership. San Francisco, Calif: Jossey-Bass/ John Wiley & Sons.

Goleman, Daniel. (1995). Emotional Intelligence: Why It Can Matter More Than Iq. New York: Bantam Books, 1995.

Greenleaf, Robert K. (1977). Servant Leadership: A Journey Into the Nature of Legitimate Power and Greatness. New York: Paulist Press.

Gunykunst, W. & Ting-Toomey, S. (1988). Culture and Affective Communication. California: Sage Publications.

King, Martin L. (1964). Why We Can't Wait. New York: Harper Collins.

Maxwell, J. C. (2007). The 21 irrefutable laws of leadership: Follow them and people will follow you. New York, NY: HarperCollins.

Myers, Ken. (2016). What Is Culture? www.thegospelcoalition.com

Northouse, Peter Guy. (2019) Leadership: Theory and Practice. (Eighth Edition). Los Angeles: SAGE Publications.

Rogers, Carl R. (1961). On becoming a person . Boston: Houghton Mifflin.

Romano, Aja. (2019). Why we can't stop fighting about cancel culture

Is cancel culture a mob mentality, or a long overdue way of speaking truth to power? DC: Vox.

Roosevelt, Theodore, and Brian Thomsen. (2003). The Man in the Arena: The Selected Writings of Theodore Roosevelt ; a Reader. New York: Forge.

Sandberg, S., & Grant, A. M. (2017). Option B: Facing adversity, building resilience, and finding joy (First edition.). New York: Knopf Doubleday.

Shakespeare, William, and Russ McDonald. (2001).The Tragedy of Othello, the Moor of Venice. New York: Penguin Books.

Sue, Derald Wing. (2010). Microaggressions in Everyday Life: Race, Gender and Sexual Orientation. New Jersey. Wiley & Sons.

Williams, Raymond. (1958). Culture and Society, 1780–1950. New York: Columbia University Press.

Williamson, Marianne. (1992). A Return to Love: Reflections on the Principles of a Course in Miracles. New York: Harper Collins.

Zimmermann, K. (2017). What is Culture? www.livescience.com

WEB LINKS

https://emtrain.com/blog/workplace-culture/2020-trends-watch/

https://geerthofstede.com/culture-geert-hofstede-gert-jan-hofstede/6d-model-of-national-culture/

http://oneracemovement.com/

https://www.pewresearch.org/search/Millennials

https://www.sapiens.org/category/culture/

https://www.ted.com/talks/thomas_curran_our_dangerous_ob-
session_with_perfectionism_is_getting_worse

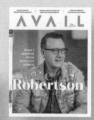

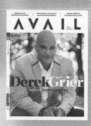

AVAIL LEADERSHIP PODCAST

WITH VIRGIL SIERRA